# CULP'S HILL

BATTLEGROUND AMERICA GUIDES offer a unique approach to the battles and battlefields of America. Each book in the series highlights a small American battlefield—sometimes a small portion of a much larger battlefield. All of the units, important individuals, and actions of each engagement on the battlefield are described in a clear and concise narrative. Historical images and modern-day photographs tie the dramatic events of the past to today's battlefield site and highlight the importance of terrain in battle. The present-day battlefield is described in detail with suggestions for touring the site.

BATTLEGROUND AMERICA

# CULP'S HILL

## The Attack and Defense of the Union Flank, July 2, 1863

John D. Cox

DA CAPO PRESS
A Member of the Perseus Books Group

Photos courtesy of: U.S. Army Military History Institute—17,
28, 50, 62, 68, 75, 78, 80, 81, 84; National Archives—30, 67, 87;
Library of Congress—33, 93, 150, 165. All other photos courtesy
of the author.

Maps by Theodore P. Savas

Cataloging-in-Publication data for this book is available from
the Library of Congress.

ISBN 0–306–81234–7
Published by Da Capo Press
A Member of the Perseus Books Group
http://www.dacapopress.com

Da Capo Press books are available at special discounts for bulk
purchases in the U.S. by corporations, institutions, and other
organizations. For more information, please contact the Special
Markets Department at the Perseus Books Group, 11 Cambridge
Center, Cambridge, MA 02142, or call (617) 252–5298.

1 2 3 4 5 6 7 8 9—05 04 03

To my Mother
Betty Cox
Whose stories of Lee and Jackson
inspired my passion for our American Civil War

# ACKNOWLEDGMENTS

No one writes a book alone, thus it is appropriate to thank those who have helped. First and foremost, I would like to thank the Gettysburg Licensed Battlefield Guides. No group or individual comes even remotely close to the knowledge and expertise of the Battlefield Guides at Gettysburg. They are simply the best and I am honored to be one of them. All of my Guide colleagues helped, though they may not realize it; however, a few need to be singled out. Jim Clouse and Ed Guy helped me to figure out the system at the National Archives, even though I still do not understand it. Jim's knowledge of the records contained in the National Archives is legendary. A special thanks is truly deserved, also, for Donny Walters, without whose assistance I would have never been able to pass the Guide exams. Donny has taught me more about the great battle than anyone has, if one can get by his bad jokes. Recognition is due to Tony Nicastro for "Varus, Varus, where are my Legions?" and to Alan Crawford for his insightful and thoughtful conversations. Gratefulness is also extended to Howie Frankenfield, Wayne Motts, Mike Phipps, Chris Rebman, Tim Smith, and Tim Krapf.

The greatest thanks, however, go to Dr. Charles C. Fennell, who has taught me more about the fighting at Culp's Hill than anyone. This is appropriate because no one knows more about Culp's Hill than Charlie does. Charlie's character as a human being, however, exceeds his knowledge of George Sears Greene and the struggle for the hill. He truly is one of the finest people I know.

Special gratitude is extended to Steve Anderson for his tireless efforts in proofreading my manuscript and offering sound advice. I must also thank Ken Lindberg for his quiet patience and guidance. Praise is also extended to my good friend Lance Herdegen for his inspiration and direction and also to my editor, Ted Savas. Ted gently applied pressure as my manuscript became later and later, and always knew how to motivate me.

Last of all, and most definitely not the least, I would like to thank my wife, Barbara, without whose assistance I would accomplish nothing. Everything is possible because of you.

# CONTENTS

# INTRODUCTION

GETTYSBURG WAS THE LARGEST BATTLE ever fought in the Western Hemisphere. It is also the most written about. Edwin Coddington, who wrote the epic one-volume account of the battle, called Gettysburg "a fatal attraction for historians." For if one is to study American history, that person will inevitably walk down a road that leads to the tiny village in south central Pennsylvania. It is no wonder then that Gettysburg conjures up all kinds of emotions in the hearts of Americans (as well as foreigners), and for all the words pressed into print over 140 some years, there are still more being published every day. The fascination with Gettysburg never ends.

Yet, with all that has been written about the great battle, it is utterly amazing to discover that certain actions of it are ignored or forgotten. The names of places like Little Round Top, the Devil's Den, the Wheatfield, and Cemetery Ridge easily invoke images to even the casual observer. Over and over again, historians write books about the strategy of the campaign and the tactics of the battlefield. One could readily stock an entire home library with information on "Lee's mistakes at Gettysburg." That is, if one believes Lee made mistakes at all; if not, one could fill his or her entire basement with literature on how Jeb Stuart lost the campaign by not showing up at all. If your tastes are not the "hell bent for leather" type and you prefer the foot soldier, the documents are infinite. Lieutenant General James Longstreet could be your guy. Longstreet is accused of losing the battle by disobeying Lee's orders and not executing his boss's plans properly. Or is it that Lee lost the battle by not listening to Longstreet's advice to "move around the right"? Could it be, finally, that Lieutenant General Richard S. Ewell's failure to attack Cemetery Hill on July 1 cost the Confederates the victory they so desperately needed? Lost somewhere in all the analysis on the Confederate side is the echo of a statement by the ill-fated hero of the famous charge, Major General George E. Pickett, who once said, "I always thought the Yankees had something to do with it." Because Gettysburg is a never-ending passion for me, personally I think it's wonderful. May the words and debates continue!

This narrative will cover controversies where applicable, some, albeit briefly. Readers should investigate further all matters concerning Gettysburg, or the war, by doing their own research.

However, it is tragic that the fighting that occurred on Culp's Hill is consistently glossed over and given only the slightest mention, if at all. Its neglect has caused even the best of the Gettysburg historians to misunderstand the battle. Sometimes this oversight seems amazing. After hundreds and hundreds of detailed pages describing the fighting on the south end of the field, an author will write only one or two sentences on Culp's Hill. The battle of Gettysburg, to be succinct, would have been a defeat for Union arms if not for the fortitude and courage of those men who defended Culp's Hill on the night of July 2. No accounting of the battle is credible or complete without an understanding of this.

The aim of this work is to focus specifically on Culp's Hill on the evening of July 2, 1863. It will follow the men and their commanders in this epic struggle, giving background as needed. It is not intended to be the classic, definitive study of the fighting on Culp's Hill, but will at least give those who are interested a better understanding of what happened there. For those who want more depth on the subject it is recommended that they read Dr. Harry W. Pfanz's book *Gettysburg: Culp's Hill & Cemetery Hill*. Dr. Pfanz's work is simply the best there is.

So why write anything further about it? The answer to that question is that, despite all that's been written about Gettysburg, more still needs to be said about the fighting on Culp's Hill on July 2, 1863.

# 1

## THE CONFEDERATES
## MOVE INTO BATTLE

SUNDAY, THE 28TH OF JUNE, 1863, WAS A DAY of immense importance. In the evening, while resting his troops at Chambersburg, Lieutenant General James Longstreet received a visitor. It was none other than his scout, or spy, known only at the time as Harrison. Longstreet wrote of the information provided to him by this one-time actor turned intelligence gatherer:

> He told me he had been to Washington and had spent his gold freely, drinking the saloons and getting upon confidential terms with army officers. In that way he had formed a pretty good idea of the general movements of the Federal army and the preparation to give us battle. The moment he heard [General Joseph] Hooker had started across the Potomac he set out to find me. He fell in with the Federal army before reaching Frederick—his plan being to walk at night and stop during the day in the neighborhood of the troops. He said there were three corps near Frederick when he passed there, one to the right and one to the left, but he did not succeed in getting the position of the other. This information proved more accurate than we could have expected if we had been relying upon our cavalry.

Longstreet then had Harrison repeat the story to General Lee, who was much distressed after hearing the report. For one thing, he did not like the manner in which he received the news, from a man about whom he knew nothing. This caused Lee to wonder where in the world Jeb Stuart could be and why he had not told him that the Federal army had crossed the Potomac. The reality Lee faced was that the Confederate army would have to change tactics. Lee had scattered his army about the countryside in order to be more effective at foraging for supplies. This was quite a risk for him to take if the Union army caught him off guard. Deep in the enemy's country and spread thinly, his forces could be destroyed in detail, or in other terms, one part at a time. It was evident that Lee's army could no longer continue their massive raid of the countryside, so they would have to concentrate their forces and prepare to do battle.

Lee was concerned about a possible advance of the Army of the Potomac into the Cumberland Valley. A movement of this nature, west into the valley, could possibly cut his lines of communication with Virginia. Therefore, in order to protect his link with his home base, he decided to concentrate his forces east of the South Mountain range. Thus, the Army of Northern Virginia needed to vacate the Cumberland Valley and find a place to consolidate. The Cashtown and Gettysburg area was perfectly situated for this purpose. The existing road network to Gettysburg alone was like the spokes on a wheel. Not less than ten roads led there, thus producing travel routes that could avoid congestion and facilitate rapidity of movement. Longstreet's and Hill's forces needed merely to travel directly east on the Chambersburg Pike to reach either Cashtown or Gettysburg. Lee then issued orders for General Richard Stoddert Ewell to stop his advance on Harrisburg, giving him the choice of marching to either town. Future developments, however, would determine Ewell's movements for him.

**Lieutenant General Richard S. Ewell**

Lee's orders to his commanders directing them to concentrate also stipulated not to bring on a general engagement. Lee was not sure of the precise location of all Federal units. He was seriously concerned that a detached unit in his army, while on the move, could initiate a battle. Isolated, beyond support, the unit might be destroyed. It was imperative that his army be fully up, or concentrated, before any shooting started. Therefore, Lee's orders to all commanders were to concentrate in the Gettysburg/Cashtown area, but avoid a fight.

On June 29, Ewell, complying with Lee's orders, sent his corps in motion. He dispatched Major General Edward Johnson's division, along with the Second Corps' massive wagon train, down the Cumberland Valley. Johnson was to backtrack, following his route of invasion, south toward Chambersburg. He could then approach the point of concentration from the west. Ewell's other two divisions, those of Generals Rodes and Early, headed south on parallel roads in the direction of Cashtown. Ewell would travel with Rodes's division.

About 9:00 A.M. on July 1, Ewell received a message from Lieutenant General A. P. Hill informing him that Hill was moving to Gettysburg. It is to Ewell's credit that he immediately redirected Rodes and Early to march there, too. Johnson's division, taking a more circuitous route, however, would have a much harder time reaching Gettysburg. Ewell sent his stepson, Major Campbell Brown, to find Lee and tell him of the corps' movement.

By the time Ewell received Hill's note, the battle had begun. In essence, Major General Henry Heth, with Hill's approval, disobeyed Lee's orders and started shooting at dismounted Union cavalry on his way to Gettysburg. Termed a meeting engagement, both sides essentially ran into each other and the fight was on. The battle of Gettysburg on July 1 seemed to have a mind of its own. It would grow larger and larger, as both sides rushed more troops to the field. Its story is a heroic epic but can be covered only briefly as pertains to this narrative.

Ewell directed Rodes to advance his division toward Gettysburg along a high, long rise, known as Oak Ridge. They brushed aside Union cavalry skirmishers, which were more a nuisance than a real danger. Soon they arrived on Oak Hill with a full panoramic view of the morning's battle. Ewell instructed Lieutenant Colonel Thomas Carter to unlimber his four batteries and get to work. Still under orders not to bring on a general engagement, Ewell nonetheless perceived the present situation as a threat. The Union First Corps, which had bashed heads with Hill earlier, was to his front and right. Howard's Eleventh Corps was approaching from the plain, north of town, to his left. There was only one thing for the one-legged, balding, newly appointed Lieutenant General to do—attack! In the style of old "Blue Light," his former commander "Stonewall Jackson," Ewell became the aggressor.

It wasn't quite like a classic Jackson assault with alacrity, as Ewell began his attack. The bulk of Rodes's division, four of five brigades, was to sweep the Yankees from Oak Ridge, while one brigade was to hold the Eleventh Corps in check, until Early arrived from the east. General John C.

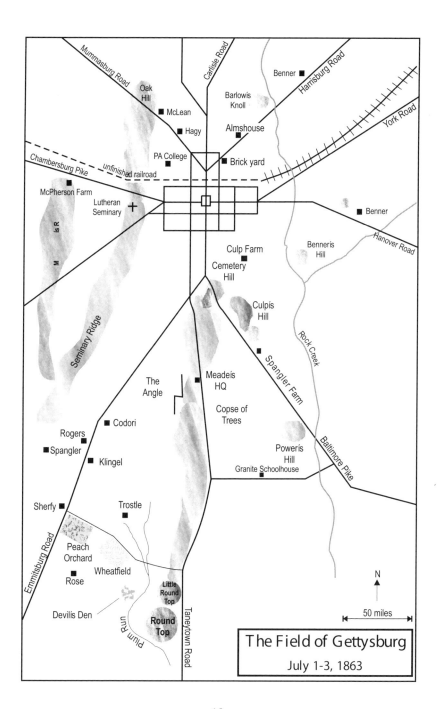

The Field of Gettysburg

July 1-3, 1863

Robinson's division of the Union First Corps defended the position along Oak Ridge, and they would prove tough adversaries. Rodes's plan to assail them was ill prepared, however, and his uncoordinated offensive failed tragically. Robinson stopped O'Neal's Alabama Brigade in its tracks and quickly changed front to the left, annihilating Iverson's North Carolinians. Even though it was a disaster, Rodes would not give up. He committed the remainder of his brigades in the afternoon and finally dislodged Robinson's Yankees in one of the bloodiest encounters of the battle.

Ewell, meanwhile, sent Brigadier General George Doles's Georgia Brigade to the left of Oak Hill to delay the approach of the Yankees. This they did, barely holding off Yankee efforts to overlap them, as they skirmished with various units of the Eleventh Corps. Patiently they fought on, awaiting the appearance of Early's division. When Early did arrive, his timing could not have been more perfect. Early launched a devastating attack on the Yankee right flank, from the Harrisburg Road, that almost totally obliterated the Eleventh Corps.

At a time during the battle, Ewell, who witnessed the beginning of Rodes's attack on Oak Hill, rode off to the east, probably as Early was driving the Federals back. A shell fragment hit his horse in the head and Ewell went flying, violently to the ground. Fortunately for the general, he recovered quickly.

At about this same moment, Hill's men pressured the First Corps on the Union left. It was too much to bear. The entire Yankee force began to give way in a retreat that appeared on the verge of a rout. All that remained was to follow up the gains of the day with continued aggressive pursuit.

For Ewell, this moment would be his worst, leaving him forever entangled in possibly the greatest controversy of Gettysburg, and arguably the war. He seems a tragic figure, comical in physical appearance and berated, sometimes unmercifully by his critics. The events surrounding this controversy are not hard to illustrate—they are merely facts.

The challenge, however, is to sort through and piece together all the reliable sources analyzing Ewell's actions. Succinctly put, the Confederates did well on the first day, driving the Yankees back, but then they failed to follow it up by attacking Cemetery Hill. Ewell is the central figure in the drama. It seems only natural to partially cover the debate of Cemetery Hill, though to go too far is to step into a quagmire and sink.

More importantly for the purpose of this book, and generally not so scrutinized as Cemetery Hill, is that the Confederates also failed to occupy Culp's Hill on July 1. Cemetery Hill is always linked with Culp's Hill.

Earlier in the day, as mentioned, Ewell sent Campbell Brown to deliver a message to Lee. Lee was at Cashtown, a short distance away, and Brown returned quickly, bearing a reminder from the commander. Ewell wrote in his Official Report:

> I notified the general commanding of my movements, and was informed by him that, in case we found the enemy's force very large, he did not want a general engagement brought on till the rest of the army came up.

It should be an established fact at this point that this was a battle that General Lee did not want. Ewell continued:

> By the time this message reached me, General A. P. Hill had already been warmly engaged with a large body of the enemy... It was too late to avoid an engagement without abandoning the position already taken up, and I determined to push the attack vigorously.

Ewell sounded like Jackson, and acted like him, attacking immediately upon arriving on the field. He was showing initiative. Early's flank attack had slammed the right of the

Eleventh Corps and the Yankees were retreating in disarray through the town. The Confederates were fast on their heels, capturing the slow, wounded, and misfortunate ones as they pursued. Ewell watched the action on a hill, in the plain north of the town.

Early's division consisted of four brigades and he had used three of them heavily to drive the Yankees from the field. Brigadier General John B. Gordon's brigade had been the first to encounter the enemy and they drove them back about a half-mile, near the Almshouse. Early halted them when he perceived the Yankees forming a new line. This line he attacked with Brigadier General Harry Hays's and Colonel Isaac Avery's brigades. Early's division was becoming used up. Though the Confederates were decidedly winning, their casualties were mounting. Ewell reported, "My loss on this day was less than 2,900 killed, wounded, and missing." The bloodied and demoralized Union troops were rallying on Cemetery Hill and Ewell, with those officers around him, could see it. The question presently in the air was how and with what troops could Cemetery Hill be assaulted.

Johnson's division was about an hour's march away and Ewell could have certainly put them to good effect at this moment. From his perch on the hill, Ewell received a messenger from Johnson, Major Henry Kyd Douglas. Douglas wrote of the moment:

> Hearing that fighting was going on in the vicinity of Gettysburg, Johnson pushed on with vigor in that direction; he seemed to be spoiling for a fight with his new division—Jackson's own. It is six miles from Cashtown to Gettysburg and before we had finished little more than half of the distance General Johnson directed me to ride rapidly to General Ewell and say to him that he was marching on Gettysburg, rapidly, with his division in prime condition and was ready to put it in as soon as he got there.

I changed to "Dick Turpin," my Milroy horse, in a twinkling and with a courier was off. I reached General Ewell without the courier, and found him with a group of officers on a hill, looking at Gettysburg and the surroundings. One of these officers was Brigadier General John B. Gordon, fresh from his part of the fight of the afternoon. I gave General Ewell my message and tried to express General Johnson's earnestness as well as I could. When I finished General Gordon seemed to second it, saying that he could join in the attack with his brigade and they could carry that hill—pointing to Cemetery Hill—before dark.

So, Johnson's division was on the move and could be expected soon, but how soon was imperative. If a continued push onto Cemetery Hill were to be made, it would have to be with the tired, battle-fatigued troops at hand or with reinforcements from A. P. Hill. Unless, of course, Johnson's fresh division could arrive soon. Ewell has been said to have pondered the situation in silence. Then, he turned to Douglas and told him to have Johnson halt at the front and wait for further instructions when he arrived. He also made a statement that he thought Lee was at Cashtown, though he was not. Lee was probably at or around Herr's Ridge, about two miles from Gettysburg. Ewell proceeded then to say, "He (Lee) directed me to come to Gettysburg, and I have done so. I do not feel like going further or making an attack without orders from him." Now, so the legend goes, Major Sandie Pendleton of Ewell's staff, remarked, "Oh, for the presence and inspiration of Old Jack for just one hour!"

The Confederates were taking the town and Ewell followed them. At the square, he sat on his horse and again, seemed to be pensive. Captain James Power Smith joined Ewell and told him General Lee was nearby, at Seminary Ridge. While these two men conversed, Major Walter H.

Taylor, from Lee's staff, arrived with an order from the commanding general. Taylor wrote in his work *Four Years with General Lee* about meeting Ewell by the square in town. He says:

> General Lee witnessed the flight of the Federals through Gettysburg and up the hills beyond. He then directed me to go to General Ewell and to say to him that, from the position which he occupied, he could see the enemy retreating over those hills, without organization and in great confusion, that it was only necessary to press "those people" in order to secure possession of the heights, and that, if possible, he wished him to do this. In obedience to these instructions, I proceeded immediately to General Ewell.

Ewell gave Taylor a message that concerned the number of prisoners captured during the day's fighting and Taylor went off to deliver it to Lee. About 3,600 Union men had become captives and Ewell was in charge of overseeing most of them. About General Lee's order, Ewell stated it instructed him "to attack this hill, if I could do so to advantage." Lee remembered it this way: "General Ewell was therefore instructed to carry the hill occupied by the enemy if he found it practicable, but to avoid a general engagement until the arrival of the other divisions of the army which were ordered to hasten forward." So, Taylor's version is somewhat different than Lee's and Ewell's.

Ewell remained in the square and took care of administrative business with his staff nearby. Many of them were filled with anxiety as the clock ticked, giving the Yankees precious time to solidify their defenses. Ewell had asked for Rodes and Early to consult with him over the current circumstances. He seemed to be in no hurry and was content to wait. Shortly, the two generals appeared and told Ewell that their men had passed through the town and now stood at the edge of Cemetery Hill. They needed only to be given the command from Ewell, with support on the right, to storm the heights. Ewell turned to James Power Smith and asked him to repeat what he had heard to Lee, requesting reinforcements from A. P. Hill. Smith rode away with the information.

Early and Ewell decided to do some personal reconnoitering and rode down Baltimore Street. Suddenly, bullets zipped and whizzed around them. The Yankees had them in range and it was becoming a bit too dangerous. The generals' investigation was thorough enough and they decided it best to find safety. Their examination was not positive. Union forces were dug in behind stone walls and at least forty guns lined the crest, their muzzles like open mouths poised to spew death upon those willing to challenge their presence.

Smith returned and brought them more bad news; Lee had no troops to offer, Ewell must attack with the men at hand. But what troops were available, after the heavy fighting of the day? Of the two divisions Ewell had available, Early's was the logical choice. They had suffered much fewer casualties, about 500, compared to Rodes's losses of approximately 2,500. Meanwhile, there was an added problem of a reported threat to the left flank and rear from Brigadier General "Extra" Billy Smith. Smith said an enemy force was moving on the York Pike, advancing upon them. Ewell did not believe the threat credible, but caution was better than negligence. Two of Early's brigades, Gordon's and Smith's, were sent to guard against the supposed risk. Early, therefore, had only two brigades for use in an attack.

Lee again, reported Major Smith, stated not to bring on a general engagement, however, until the army was fully up and concentrated. Ewell wrote in his Official Report his reasoning for not attacking Cemetery Hill: "I could not bring artillery to bear on it, and all the troops with me were jaded by twelve hours' marching and fighting." Also, Ewell continued, Johnson's division did not arrive soon enough to be placed in a position to execute an assault and the hill "was not assailable from the town." Ewell did not really give up on the prospect of controlling Cemetery Hill, he just believed there was another way of gaining it. He set his sights on an alternative means of dislodging the Union forces ensconced on the formidable heights: Take control of Culp's Hill!

It would be an unnecessary waste of lives to try a brutal frontal assault that quite possibly could fail, leaving his command in a weakened position. The key to the position lay to the southeast, in the rear of Cemetery Hill, a mere 800 yards away. It is no wonder that Ewell took his time—he still believed Culp's Hill was open. Consider the following in his report:

> Cemetery Hill was not assailable from the town, and I determined, with Johnson's division, to take possession of a wooded hill to my left, on a line with and commanding Cemetery Hill.

The hill still seemed accessible, and Ewell decided it was time to send a reconnaissance party to the area to make sure. General Johnson had arrived, but not his men. Johnson's division was about a mile from town and caught in a traffic jam, blocked up by the wagon trains of Longstreet's corps. Though, the truth of it seemed the opposite, that Longstreet's men were snared in a mass of road congestion caused by Ewell's trains. No matter, Johnson's men would be here soon and they needed to get up Culp's Hill before the Yankees fortified it. Time was of the essence, and it was best to send that scouting party on its way.

### The Confederate Reconnaissance of Culp's Hill
The reconnaissance of the Union left flank on the morning of July 2, by Captain Samuel Johnston of Lee's Engineering Corps, is said by some to have decided the outcome of the battle. Johnston reported to Lee that he rode to the top of

26

Little Round Top and did not see any Union troops. The significance, let alone the truth, of this information is debatable. Lee's attack orders for July 2 did not call for the taking of Little Round Top. In fact, Little Round Top was not even mentioned in Lee's battle plans!

A lack of interest in the Confederate reconnaissance of Culp's Hill on July 1 is a fundamental flaw when considering the Confederates' failure to achieve success in the battle. There was much more at stake in the moment and a much greater opportunity for Lee to fulfill his objectives of the campaign. Meaning, if Ewell had seized Culp's Hill promptly, as many claimed he hesitated in attacking Cemetery Hill, there would have been no second or third day of battle.

Colonel William Oates admitted in letters to Colonel E. P. Alexander after the war that he did not think he could have held Little Round Top, even if he had taken it. And there were a lot more troops, in better condition, on Little Round Top in the afternoon of July 2 than there were on Culp's Hill on the night of July 1.

At any rate, the reconnaissance of Culp's Hill is very similar to the one on Little Round Top. Both produced the same results, which amounted to false information.

Ewell sent two young Lieutenants, Thomas T. Turner and General Early's nephew, Robert Early, to reconnoiter Culp's Hill. The two rode out in the direction of Culp's Hill and claimed they reached its crest. Surprisingly, they found no Union troops and could see the enemy's entire line of battle. The two scouts must have swung far off to the left, crossed Rock Creek, and climbed the hill on its northeast or eastern side. Ascending the hill from the southeast does not seem possible, because it would have brought them into the rear of the Iron Brigade. However, their reconnaissance was aided with the darkening sky and the wooded nature of the hill. Somehow, like Captain Johnston the following morning, they avoided being seen or captured by Union forces. They rode back to inform Ewell of the news.

**A view of Culp's Hill from a nineteenth-century photograph.**

Major General Isaac Trimble, a very bitter man after the war, claimed a personal reconnaissance of Culp's Hill earlier in the day. The following excerpt is from an article written by him that appeared in the Southern Historical Society Papers in 1898.

> As no movement seemed immediate, I rode off to our left, north of the town, to reconnoitre, and noticed conspicuously the wooded hill northeast of Gettysburg, and a half mile distant, and of an elevation to command the country for miles each way, and overlooking Cemetery Hill above the town. Returning to see General Ewell, who was still under much embarrassment, I said: "General, *there*," pointing to Culp's Hill, "is an eminence of commanding position, and not now occupied, as it ought to be by us or the enemy soon. I advise you to send a brigade and hold it if we are to remain here." He said: "Are you sure it commands the town?" "Certainly it does, as you can see, and it ought to be held by us at once."

General Ewell made some impatient reply, and the conversation dropped.

General Isaac Trimble became one of the leading critics of Ewell's performance at Gettysburg. Trimble accused Ewell of being "indecisive" at Gettysburg, as his above statement exemplifies. His comments must be read carefully with an understanding of his bitterness. At Gettysburg, Trimble would lead a division in Pickett's Charge and lose a leg. He was captured and spent the remainder of the war in Federal prisons. He did not like Ewell.

The two young scouts, Thomas Turner and Robert Early, returning from their intelligence-gathering mission, found Generals Ewell, Rodes, and Early in conversation. They told the star-studded threesome what they had found.

At dusk, Johnson's men had finally reached the town and were camped by the Pennsylvania (now Gettysburg) College. Ewell asked Rodes what he thought of moving Johnson's division that very night to occupy Culp's Hill. Rodes responded by saying, "He did not think it would result in anything one way or the other." Ewell then asked Early, who responded, "If you do not go up there tonight, it will cost you 10,000 lives to get up there tomorrow." At some point—possibly after this discussion, though it is not clear—Ewell ordered Johnson to make a reconnaissance of Culp's Hill and take it if it remained unoccupied. It was dark now and valuable time had slipped away.

Johnson's men marched toward Gettysburg by turning off the Chambersburg Pike and moving into the railroad bed, coming out east of the town. Colonel Jesse Williams recorded his brigade's movement as they led the division on the march

> along the railroad, about three-quarters of a mile from town, and there, by his direction (Johnson's), was placed in line of battle on the extreme right of

**Major General
Jubal A. Early**

the division, about 600 yards from and perpendicu-
lar to the railroad.

As the men filed into line in the darkness, they faced the
heights of Culp's Hill, less than a mile away. They slept on
their arms that evening.

General Lee paid a visit to Ewell after sunset to get an
assessment of the condition of the Second Corps. Lee found
Ewell with Rodes, and an orderly was sent to find Early,
who quickly arrived. Lee was seeking the counsel of Ewell
and his officers concerning the possibilities for attack the
next day. Lee wanted to strike first thing in the morning and
he asked, "Can't you, with your Corps, attack on this flank
at daylight tomorrow?" Early spoke up and soon dominated
the discussion. To read his writings after the war, one can
easily get the impression that he, and not Ewell, was in command of the Second Corps. Early stated that he had been
through Gettysburg the week before and rode that very
afternoon, reconnoitering the ground. He felt he knew the
ground better than any officer present. He expressed the
opinion to Lee that the ground on the Union right was not
suitable for offensive operations. It was rocky, wooded, and

steep. The Federals were also dug in on Cemetery Hill and had massed their artillery. It would be a most difficult proposition to assail them. "Success in attack was doubtful." Early thought it best if Longstreet's corps was selected as the main attack force, hammering the Union left.

All seemed to agree with General Early, at least he said so in his writings in the Southern Historical Society Papers. Lee then asked, "Then perhaps I had better draw you around towards my right, as the line will be very long and thin if you remain here, and the enemy may come down and break through it?"

Early again spoke first, "On that part of the line it was more difficult for the enemy to come down from the heights to attack us than for us to ascend them to attack him, difficult as the latter would have been." Ewell and Rodes were of the same opinion. The conference ended with the decision that Longstreet would lead the main assault, striking the Union's left flank, while Ewell would make a diversionary attack against the right.

Lee left the meeting feeling bewildered. We can imagine him, on his famous horse "Traveller," riding off deep in thought. Colonel Arthur Freemantle described his first impression of him:

> General Lee is, almost without exception, the hand-somest man of his age I ever saw. He is fifty-six years old, tall, broad-shouldered, very well made, well set up—a thorough soldier in appearance; and his manners are most courteous and full of dignity. He is a perfect gentleman in every respect. I imagine no man has so few enemies, or is universally esteemed. Throughout the South, all agree in pronouncing him to be as near perfection as a man can be.

Not much is said about Lee's personal life during the Gettysburg Campaign, probably because Lee rarely talked about it. But his health was failing; in the first week of April

1863, Douglas Southall Freeman, Lee's esteemed biographer, wrote

> He had not been sleeping well, and in some way he
> contracted a serious throat infection which settled
> into what seems to have been a pericarditis. His
> arm, his chest, and his back were attacked with
> sharp paroxysms of pain that suggest even the possibility of an angina.

Freeman's diagnosis seems to point to the possibility of a mild heart attack. Lee's wife, Mary Anne Randolph Custis, was of ill health since the 1850s and needed care. To compound his problems, his second son, William Henry Fitzhugh "Rooney" Lee, had been captured on June 9 at the Battle of Brandy Station during the campaign. Northern authorities were threatening to hang him in retaliation for an obscure incident in Kentucky. General Ambrose Burnside had just executed two Confederates in the "Bluegrass State" for recruiting behind Union lines. The South was indignant and threatened to retaliate by hanging two Union prisoners in kind. When the news reached Washington, Federal authorities announced that if the Confederacy persisted in this manner, they would institute an "eye-for-eye" policy. "Rooney" Lee was one of the Confederates selected to be hanged. Soon, tempers died down and eventually, on February 25, 1864, "Rooney" Lee was exchanged.

It has been noted that during the Battle of Gettysburg, Lee may have suffered from an illness common to Civil War soldiers—diarrhea. Yet, he was a commanding figure, whose sheer presence would inspire his men to fits of hysteria.

Riding away from the meeting with generals of his Second Corps, Lee was perplexed. He had spoken with Longstreet, his "old Warhorse," during the day and Longstreet advocated a move around the Union right—a

**General Robert E. Lee**

flanking maneuver, not an attack. Ewell and his subordinates also did not seem willing to take the offense on their front. The great Army of Northern Virginia, a machine Lee had molded into an efficient instrument of killing, was doubting and unwilling to carry through on the efforts won on this day. Did Lee think of Jackson? Did he wish that "Stonewall" was with him, here at Gettysburg? If he did, certainly he must have felt that Jackson would have been recommending, even thirsting, for a strike at the punch-drunk foe. We do not know if Lee thought of Jackson, though many Second Corps officers claimed that they did. Hence, the supposed statement of Sandie Pendleton, asking for the inspiration of Jackson for just one hour. After the war, on February 19, 1870, Colonel William Allan, an officer of the Second Corps, would claim that Lee said to him, "if Jackson had been there (Gettysburg) he would have succeeded."

Lee was not a man that overtaxed his mind with melancholy thoughts; he was a man of action. He sent a note to Ewell, changing the plans discussed in their meeting. Lee stated that unless Ewell thought that the Second Corps could gain an advantage on their front, they would be better utilized moving to the Confederate right, because an attack in that sector seemed more likely to succeed.

Ewell did not agree. He decided to ride to Lee's headquarters to meet personally with the commanding general. Ewell explained that Culp's Hill was still unoccupied and that that, in and of itself, gave the Second Corps great advantage on its front. Lee assented, as long as Ewell was going to attack, or occupy Culp's Hill, his troops would remain as the Confederate left flank. It was agreed. The original plan of attack was to be executed. Longstreet was to strike the left, while Ewell attacked the right.

Ewell rode back to his headquarters and summoned Lieutenant Turner and asked him to tell Johnson to occupy Culp's Hill immediately, if he had not done so already. Turner went off to find Johnson. It was about midnight.

Johnson had previously formed a reconnaissance party to investigate the status of the hill. The size of this band of intelligence-gatherers and who was in charge of it is not known. The outcome of it, however, is clear.

The 7th Indiana, which was part of the First Corps, was guarding wagon trains earlier in the day and arrived at Gettysburg later, missing the action. The regiment's commander, Colonel Ira Glover, was ordered by General Wadsworth to extend the line of the Iron Brigade, on Culp's Hill. Colonel Glover wrote, "We immediately commenced the construction of a temporary breastwork." Company B of the regiment was posted as pickets forward of the breastwork and a little to the right, on the east slope of the hill. Hence, on the evening of July 1 the Iron Brigade was the right of the Union line, followed by the 7th Indiana.

One of the most forgotten but significant moments of the Battle of Gettysburg now occurred. Luckily, the incident was well recorded by one participant, a soldier in Company B. He stated that the pickets initially deployed "to the south, along the base of the ridge and in front of the position occupied during the 2d and 3d days of July by the

Twelfth Corps. For some unexplained reason, this line of pickets was withdrawn and the line shortened to within a few yards of the right of our line of battle." Colonel Glover wrote, "During the succeeding night a force of the enemy attempted to penetrate our lines, but were easily driven off, supposing themselves confronted by a heavy force."

Johnson sent men ahead of his division to see if Culp's Hill was vacant. They ran into Company B. Amazingly, one company held off Johnson's entire division! Yes, technically speaking, it was true. A soldier of the company wrote:

> The enemy, in carrying out his purpose to attack, advanced a division of troops to and across Rock Creek, detachments of which were thrown out in advance to feel our lines. The hour was about 11 p.m.
>
> Serg't Hussey and private Harshbarger were our extreme right pickets. A noise was heard as of men moving cautiously in the timber some distance to our right. As we advanced to investigate, before the enemy discovered us, we got behind some obstructions, permitting the officer in command of the party to pass us, when Serg't Hussey dashed out and seized the officer, while Harshbarger fired upon the advancing body of troops. Other members of our company running up, poured in such a rapid fire that the enemy turned and fled, leaving some prisoners in our hands.

Much on Culp's Hill would ultimately be decided by darkness. One company of troops, placed in a most fortuitous position, foiled the plans of the entire Confederate army.

The soldier continued:

> The vigilance exercised upon this occasion caused the enemy to conclude that we "fully occupied the

h(e)ights," when, as a matter of fact, the entire line to our right, in front of the division formed for this assault, was exposed, unoccupied, and open for the enemy to march right in.

Oh, for the presence of Jeb Stuart, never mind Jackson! It is understandable from the preceding passages why Civil War battles hardly ever took place at night.

The Confederates had lost a golden opportunity to gain Culp's Hill. They failed by hesitating, by the onset of darkness, and by the efforts of Company B, 7th Indiana. The capture of Culp's Hill on July 1, 1863, would have rendered the Union position on Cemetery Hill untenable, thus avoiding their subsequent defeat in the following days. The soldier of Company B added, "It is, therefore, manifest that on the courage and the faithfulness of these few the safety of thousands pended." Consequently, Ewell and his Second Corps would launch bloody and futile attacks in an attempt to evict the Union from both hills.

As Ewell received the disturbing news about Johnson's failed excursion, there was added alarm. On falling back from their sortie on the hill, Johnson's men captured a Union courier! The courier carried a note from the headquarters of the Fifth Corps, stating that the corps was at Bonaughtown, just four miles away! It would be marching toward Gettysburg, and ultimately Ewell's flank, starting at 4 A.M. Ewell must have felt like the world had just crashed down on his bald spot.

Ewell has been a leading scapegoat for the Confederate defeat at Gettysburg. Trimble led the way criticizing him, but he was not the only one. Many of the officers of the Second Corps blamed Ewell and, like the statement of Sandie Pendleton, cried out for Stonewall Jackson. Edwin Coddington in his classic account of the battle was the first of the modern historians to challenge the view of Ewell as an objection of ridicule. Harry Pfanz wrote a brilliant essay in *The Gettysburg Nobody Knows*, edited by Gabor Boritt, which critically analyzes Ewell's performance in the battle and concludes favorably for "Old Bald Head." Pfanz's son, Donald, has also written an excellent biography on Ewell, which must be called the "definitive study" of the general's life. It is also positive concerning Ewell's actions.

This author concludes that with the information available, it appears Richard S. Ewell performed his duties wisely on July 1 at Gettysburg. There is entirely too much attention paid to so-called Confederate mistakes during the battle. Lee made mistakes in other battles and still won. His gambles at Chancellorsville could have resulted in utter disaster for his army. Instead, he won and it's called brilliant. It is a simple truth that at Gettysburg the common Union soldier decided that Bobby Lee would not whip him on his home turf.

# 2

# THE KEY TO THE BATTLE

THE DEFENSE OF THE TOWN on July 1, 1863, cost Union forces a great deal. Thousands were killed and wounded, while the weak and slow of foot were captured. Most significant, for the sake of the Army of the Potomac, was the loss of Major General John F. Reynolds. Reynolds was killed early in the fighting, leading the Iron Brigade into the fray. Major General Oliver Otis Howard, normally the Commander of the Union Eleventh Corps, was thus forced into command of the troops on the field. Howard had seen the importance of the high ground of Cemetery Hill upon his arrival at Gettysburg in the mid-morning hours. Riding along Cemetery Ridge south of the town, Howard naturally rode to the highest point, Cemetery Hill. Harry Pfanz in his classic account, *Gettysburg: Culp's Hill & Cemetery Hill*, gives us a terrific story. Conferring with Lieutenant Colonel Theodore A. Meysenburg, adjutant general of the Eleventh Corps, Howard remarked, "This seems to be a good position, colonel," to which Meysenburg replied, "It is the only position, general." Pfanz titles a whole chapter in his work "The Only Position."

Meysenburg and Pfanz could not have been more accurate. Cemetery Hill was the key to the Union position at Gettysburg. In warfare there are three levels that must be satisfied to insure a successful campaign: strategic, tactical, and operational. Cemetery Hill fulfills all three requirements. Strategically, the importance of defending Cemetery Hill for Union arms cannot be overemphasized. To fully appreciate this matter, it is necessary to examine the letter attached to the order appointing Major General George Gordon Meade to command of the army by the general-in-chief, Henry W. Hallack. Halleck's letter reads as follows:

> Your army is free to act as you may deem proper under the circumstances as they arise. You will, however, keep in view the important fact that the Army of the Potomac is the covering army of Washington as well as the army of operation against the invading forces of the rebels. You will, therefore, maneuver and fight in such a manner as to cover the capital and also Baltimore, as far as circumstances will admit. Should General Lee move upon either of these places, it is expected that you will either anticipate him or arrive with him so as to give him battle.

Simply, Meade was to ensure the safety of Washington, D.C., and Baltimore, while giving Lee battle. A quick glance at a map of the Gettysburg area reveals that at least ten roads lead into the town. Hence, Gettysburg is often called a "crossroads town." During the battle the Confederates gained control of eight of those roads, while the Union maintained possession of the remaining two. These two roads lead to Washington and Baltimore, and both converge on Cemetery Hill. The loss of the hill, therefore, would also include the loss of these vital roads and open the door for a Confederate advance on the Union's capital, or Baltimore. Thus, by defending Cemetery Hill, Meade is fulfilling Halleck's strategic requirements as expressed in the letter.

Tactically, Cemetery Hill is, again, critical. Overnight on July 1 and into the morning of July 2, Union forces began to concentrate on the battlefield. Using Cemetery Hill as a focal point, the Union line began to take the shape of a giant, upside down and backward "J," what is more commonly referred to as "the fishhook." The shank of the hook, to the left of Cemetery Hill, ran in a straight line in a north–south direction along Cemetery Ridge, with the left flank resting on Little Round Top. Slightly to the southeast of Cemetery Hill, the Union line bent back and ended on Culp's Hill, the barb of the hook. With both flanks resting on high ground and approximately 93,000 troops compacted into this three-mile line, the "fishhook" was a very formidable defensive position indeed.

The Confederate line simply mirrored the Union line, although it was occupied by fewer men and covered a distance about twice as long in length.

Much has been said about the positive aspects of the "fishhook" line, but very little attention has been paid to the negative. For instance, because the Union line is curved in nature—a semi-circle in its northern extremity, if you will—it allowed Union forces to be rushed to any threatened section of the line faster than if their line was straight. However, paradoxically, the strength of the line also presented its biggest weakness. The curvature of the line could expose it to crossfire or enfilade. Colonel Edward Porter Alexander described the position of the two lines in his "Military Memoirs of a Confederate," as follows:

[T]he weakest portion of their line was Cemetery Hill, and the point of greatest interest in connection with this battle is the story of our entire failure to recognize this fact... There was one single advantage conferred by our exterior lines, and but one, in exchange for many disadvantages. They gave us the opportunity to select positions for our guns which could enfilade the opposing lines of the enemy. Enfilading fire is so effective that no troops can submit to it long... What has been called the shank of the Federal fishhook, extending south from the bend at Cemetery Hill toward Little Round Top, was subject to enfilade fire from the town and its flanks and suburbs... The salient angle is acute and weak.

Finally, from an operational standpoint, Cemetery Hill was essential to the Union position at Gettysburg because it covered the Baltimore Pike, the best road available to the Federal forces. The Baltimore Pike was also the main artery of supply for the Army of the Potomac. As the fighting escalated on July 1, Union troops rushed to the scene of the action leaving their supply wagons behind. As evening cast its shadow on the battlefield and the fighting slowed to a simmer, those supply wagons were on the move to the field. In fact, the Army of the Potomac's ammunition and reserve artillery trains would be parked on the Baltimore Pike by the evening of July 2.

Although the Taneytown Road was also in the control of Union forces, the Baltimore Pike was macadamized; thus its surface was in much better condition. This meant that it constituted the Army of the Potomac's main line of retreat should disaster strike.

Succinctly stated, the occupation and defense of Cemetery Hill was the key to the Union position at Gettysburg. To take it a step further, the key to occupying and defending Cemetery Hill was Culp's Hill. Hard bitten and unreconstructed, Confederate General Jubal A. Early wrote in his "Narrative of the War Between the States":

he (Ewell) determined to move it (Johnson's Division) to a wooded hill on the left of Cemetery Hill, which seemed to command the latter hill and to be the key to the position on that flank.

The position on Cemetery Hill would be rendered untenable if Culp's Hill could not be held. Major General Daniel

E. Sickles, speaking at the dedication of the Greene Monument on September 27, 1907, at Gettysburg, described the Culp's Hill position very precisely when he said:

> If the enemy could have secured this position, which dominated Cemetery Hill, the Confederate divisions of Early, Rodes, and Pender were ready to seize that commanding height, on which their artillery would have made our line of battle on Cemetery Ridge untenable.

Rising high above Cemetery Hill, Culp's Hill did indeed "dominate" the position, but its unique geographic location, in terms of the "fishhook," made its significance even more critical. The southwestern base of Culp's Hill sat squarely on the Baltimore Pike, the Union Army's best road. Possession of Culp's Hill by Confederate forces would eliminate the use of the road for the Army of the Potomac and thus sever their line of retreat. In addition, Culp's Hill was directly situated in the Union army's rear and commanded the Cemetery Ridge line. Speaking also on the dedication of the Greene Monument, Colonel Lewis R. Stegman of the Twelfth Corps observed:

> Immediately to the southwest, within twenty minutes on the double-quick to an alert soldier, lay the headquarters of the commander-in-chief on the Taneytown Road, and the center of the Union Army, under Hancock, while directly to the rear of this brigade, across the Baltimore Pike, lay the reserve ammunition trains and reserve artillery of the Army of the Potomac, possibly five hundred yards away.

Physically, Culp's Hill is composed of two hills, which are separated by a saddle or valley in between. Both hills are wooded and strewn with car-sized and larger boulders. The heights are enclosed on the east by Rock Creek and flanked on the southwest by the Baltimore Pike. The larger height stands 180 feet above Rock Creek and the smaller 80 feet. The distance between the crest of the larger hill and the smaller one is less than a quarter mile or about four football fields. The larger hill runs in descending fashion to the smaller hill, and forms what could be called a ridge. The larger hill is north of the smaller, and as mentioned already, was about 800 yards southeast, under a half mile, from Cemetery Hill. To reach the crest of the larger hill on its northern slope is to ascend the hill complex at its steepest, which is quite a hike. The further one moves south, along the eastern side of the hill, the less steep the grade of the hill. However, it has always been covered with trees and rocks.

There are some features present in the area that had an impact on the fighting. A stone wall ran from Rock Creek toward the smaller hill, or west, and then changed direction, northwest, forming an angle, and ran up the smaller hill and into the valley. As the wall runs up the smaller hill, it goes through an open field. The field is presently named "Pardee Field," and trees bordered it. South of the smaller hill the terrain was less wooded and opens into a meadow, but is still rocky. This open area is commonly referred to as Spangler's Meadow. The meadow was, or is still, very wet and in certain areas could be called a swamp. It is about a hundred yards wide. Spangler's Spring sits in the meadow, on the south base of the smaller hill. A stream drained from the spring and ran into Rock Creek.

Rock Creek was much deeper in 1863 than it is today because there was a mill to the south of it. A dam was built to operate the mill and it made the creek deeper. The mill was owned by the McAllister family, hence it was called "McAllister's Mill." At certain points the creek could be quite a formidable obstacle to cross. Rock Creek runs in a more or less north to south direction, but begins to curve slightly toward the east about 300 yards northeast of the

Two views of Rock Creek, where Johnson's division crossed.

peak of the larger hill. The curve extends about 200 yards in an easterly direction, before bending back to the west.

Also, the Henry Spangler farm rested on the eastern side of the Baltimore Pike, about 400 yards from the hill complex. Running from the back of the Spangler buildings was a farm lane, which provided an access road into the valley between the two hills. Remnants of the lane barely exist today, but still can be found.

### "Pop" Greene

In 1635, John Greene sailed from England and settled among the Puritans of the Massachusetts Bay Colony. As the Bay Colony expanded, a series of brutal and merciless conflicts were fought against the Indians of southern New England. First, the Pequots were virtually exterminated as the Bay Colony took control of the Connecticut River valley, and later the powerful "friendly" tribe, the Narragansetts of Rhode Island, were subdued in "King Philip's War." John Greene allied himself with the exiled

**The boyhood home of George S. Greene in Apponaug, Rhode Island.**

religious radical, Roger Williams. Following Williams, Greene was one of the first to settle in the "place of the otherwise-minded," as the Puritans referred to it, Rhode Island. In 1696, nestled in a cove on Greenwich Bay, Greene helped establish the tiny village of Apponaug, within the city of Warwick. Apponaug quickly thrived as a seaport. Apponaug Cove, as it is called, gave the community access to larger population centers, like Boston, by sea as well as by land. The Greene family prospered and could claim General Nathanael Greene, the Revolutionary War hero, as a descendent. In 1796, Caleb and Sarah Greene built a home on the large tract of land that John Greene, their ancestor, had purchased from the Narragansett sachem Miantonomi (sometimes spelled Miantonomoh) in 1640. While residing at this residence Caleb and Sarah gave birth to a son on May 6, 1801. They named him George Sears Greene. George was one of nine children, five of whom survived infancy.

Caleb Greene, a successful merchant and ship owner, traded his wares internationally. His business, however, experienced a cataclysmic turn for the worse in the early nineteenth century. During the war between England and France, America tried to practice "isolationism," remaining neutral and trading freely among the warring parties. Despite the British seizure of the USS *Chesapeake*, and a declaration of a blockade of the British Isles by the French, President Thomas Jefferson continued a policy of negotiations. In 1807, Jefferson then enacted what one historian has called "the greatest experiment in search of an alternative to war in the history of the world," the Embargo Act of 1807. This law forbade all ships of the United States of America to sail to any foreign port. The result was a financial disaster for merchants, including Caleb Greene. Matters only became worse with the War of 1812, and Caleb Greene went broke.

As a result of his father's financial difficulties, young George Greene was deprived of an education at Brown

University and was forced to seek employment in a dry goods store in New York City. The young man must have been an exceptional employee as he caught the eye of the superintendent of the U.S. Military Academy at West Point, Major Sylvanus Thayer. Thayer submitted Greene's name for admission and on June 24, 1819, George S. Greene entered the academy. One of his classmates would also fight at Gettysburg, Hannibal Day. The Day and Greene families would later become in-laws through the marriage of Greene's daughter, Anna, to Day's son, Lieutenant. Murray S. Day of the United States Navy.

Four years after arriving, on July 1, 1823, Greene graduated, finished second in his class, and received a commission in the Third Regiment of Artillery. He preferred the classroom to the artillery, however, and he took an appointment as assistant professor of mathematics in September of that same year at the academy. It could not have been easy for Greene to secure such an appointment and one must assume that he was exceptional. The future general continued to teach mathematics at the academy until taking a position as assistant instructor of mathematics in the Artillery School for Practice at Fort Monroe before returning again to West Point to teach his subject.

In 1827, Second Lieutenant Greene was ordered to join his original regiment, the Third Artillery, for garrison duty at Fort Wolcott, Rhode Island. For the next half-decade Greene would serve at various posts throughout New England. In the summer of 1828, he traveled to Providence to marry Mary Elizabeth Vinton, sister of David Vinton, who finished a year ahead of Greene at West Point. The couple would have three children.

Tragedy, however, was to befall Greene, as his wife and three children all died within seven months in 1832–1833. Only a man constitutionally strong in his belief system could survive such a sad experience. Greene took to his books and began to study. In *Greene and his New York Troops at Gettysburg*, Colonel William F. Fox writes:

During the next three years he read exhaustive courses in law and medicine, qualifying himself to pass examinations admitting him to practice in either of these professions. He also continued the studies in engineering which he had pursued at all times since his graduation at West Point.

In 1835, Greene resigned his commission to pursue civil engineering. Army life in his era meant long, boring hours on desolate posts and, as was the case with Greene, very little advancement. After thirteen years of military service he had received but one promotion. Civilian life offered the opportunity for higher pay and excitement. For the next twenty years Greene worked as an engineer for various railroads. His employment took him throughout the United States, involving him in projects in Massachusetts, North Carolina, Virginia, Maryland, Kentucky, Tennessee, Maine, New York, and finally, his home state of Rhode Island.

On one of his trips to Maine, Greene met Martha Barrett Dana. Martha Dana was the daughter of the Honorable Samuel Dana, who had served in the Massachusetts Assembly and Senate and in the U.S. Congress. Martha and George married on February 21, 1837. Their marriage lasted forty-six years, ending with the death of Martha in 1883. The couple had six children, one of whom died in infancy. Three of the sons would serve in the military; one of them, Dana Greene, would be the executive officer aboard the *Monitor* during its famous fight with the *Merrimack*.

In 1856, Greene became the engineer in charge at the Department of Water Supply for New York City. While serving in this capacity Greene expanded on the existing Croton water system, designing and constructing a reservoir in Central Park, which supplied water to the city until 1991. He also supervised the enlargement of the famous High Bridge in the Bronx, which still stands over the

**Brigadier General
George S. Greene**

Harlem River and, ironically, is near Sedgwick Avenue (General Sedgwick commanded the Sixth Corps at Gettysburg). While working on these projects the country erupted into Civil War.

Greene, the father of five and sixty years of age, having not worn the uniform of a U.S. soldier for over twenty-five years, volunteered his services. The decision seemed easy for him. Greene asked for reinstatement and the government, in need of officers with experience, accepted. It was not until January 1862, however, that Greene received his command as Colonel of the 60th New York.

Colonel Fox wrote:

> The Sixtieth New York at that time was stationed near Baltimore, Md., where it had been ordered on duty as a railroad guard. Though composed of exceptionally good material, the regiment was lacking in discipline, its morale having been impaired by dissatisfaction arising from various causes. The

former colonel had just resigned in response to a written request signed by all the line officers, thus creating the vacancy to which Greene had been appointed. His arrival in camp was a surprise to all, and a disappointment to some of the officers, who would have received a promotion in case the vacancy had been filled from within the regiment.

A surprise, of course, because he was new to them, but Greene's age must have caused amazement. For most of the soldiers, he was old enough to be their father and for many, their grandfather. If any of them believed that the old man was not up to the job, Greene quickly dispelled their doubts. He called for the officers of the regiment to meet him in his tent and explained to them "in a brief address, kindly but firm in tone, . . . what he expected of them. Under his instruction the regiment made a speedy improvement in drill and discipline, and soon attained a degree of efficiency that in time made it a first-class fighting machine."

One soldier wrote this account of Greene:

> He was a West Point graduate, about sixty years old, thick set, five feet ten inches high, dark complexioned, iron-gray hair, full gray beard and mustache, gruff in manner and stern in appearance, but with all an excellent officer, and under a rough exterior possessing a kind heart. In the end the men learned to love and respect him as much as in the beginning they feared him, and this was saying a good deal on the subject. He knew how to drill, how to command, and in the hour of peril how to care for his command, and the men respected him accordingly.

Promoted to Brigadier General on April 28, 1862, Greene would see service as a staff officer and a brigade commander before finally leading a division at Antietam.

In the bloodiest single day in American history, September 17, 1862, Greene led his men in the fight over farmer Miller's now famous "Cornfield." Greene had over 1,700 men under his immediate control and he drove them forward, smashing the Confederates and advancing his division well beyond the Union army's main line. Sweeping the Cornfield, the fighting soon became hand to hand. Pressing the attack, Greene's men reached the heights of the plateau by the Dunker Church. They held this key position for over half an hour. Repeatedly the Confederates tried to dislodge them, without success. Boldly pushing the men forward again, Greene established a line 200 yards beyond and called for reinforcements, but none came. Finally, after four hours of horrific fighting, Greene's men were forced to retire as their casualties mounted and their ammunition ran low.

The men took inspiration from Greene, as he led them by example, from the front. A soldier in Greene's command wrote:

> The writer was standing close to General Greene, who was dismounted from his horse and holding the rein while directing the fighting. The fire of the enemy was terrific at this moment, when a ball struck his horse dead at his feet. The general without the least perturbation, and with the utmost coolness, deliberately took off the bridle and saddle and carried them in his arms. The enemy closed in on both flanks of the now depleted division and compelled it to fall back on the main line of battle. The General saved his saddle and bridle, and carried them back to his new battle line.

The performance by Greene and his men at the battle of Antietam was nothing less than outstanding. Greene had assessed the situation quickly and using aggressive tactics had driven the enemy back. The old man had shown great leadership in the line of fire and demonstrated his ability to command a large body of men in combat.

## Greene's New York Brigade

After the battle, Greene took his only sick leave of the war, for three weeks. Restored back to health, he reported back to the army and found it reorganized in his absence. Because of the casualties suffered during the battle of Antietam and the expiration of many enlistments, some commands had been consolidated, including Greene's. Brigadier General John White Geary had recovered from a wound he suffered in a previous battle and he outranked Greene. Therefore, Geary took command of Greene's division. Greene was essentially demoted and now found himself in command of his old brigade, the Third, of the Second Division, Twelfth Corps, Army of the Potomac. By April 1863, the unit would become know as "Greene's New York Brigade." It consisted of the 60th, 78th, 102nd, 137th and 149th New York regiments. This would be the organization that Greene would lead in the fight for Culp's Hill at Gettysburg.

The 60th New York was General Greene's first command. The 60th New York was raised way up north in the woodland counties of St. Lawrence and Franklin. Many of the men came from the town of Russell on Grasse River. The regiment was sometimes referred to as the "St. Lawrence Regiment." The men were of good common stock, being mostly farmers and laborers. At Gettysburg Colonel Abel Godard would command the regiment. He was twenty-eight years old and had studied law in Richville, New York, prior to the Civil War. He would serve the regiment honorably until discharged for disability on September 13, 1863, returning to Richville to become a real estate agent.

The 78th New York was classified as a New York City regiment, but mostly the men were from the northern part of the state—only three companies were actually raised in New York City. The bulk of the men came from the counties of Rochester, Utica, Buffalo, Bath, and Suspension Bridge. Company K was actually recruited from Michigan. The regiment was also called the "Cameron Highlanders." They were a very diverse group of men with wide ethnic backgrounds. The regiment consisted of Irish and German immigrants, as well as Canadians, Englishmen, Frenchmen, and one soldier from Australia. Their commander at Gettysburg was Lieutenant Colonel Herbert von Hammer -stein, and he, like many of the men, was born in Germany. He had experience in the Austrian army and would eventually lose his legs to frostbite while serving in the U.S. Cavalry. The regiment was somewhat lacking in discipline in the beginning of the war, but by the battle of Gettysburg, they were a good fighting unit.

The 102nd New York was recruited mostly in Manhattan and Brooklyn, although some of the men hailed from Ulster and Schoharie Counties. They also incorporated men from Ogdensburg, Lima, and Avoca, New York. Their commander was Colonel James C. Lane, who was about three weeks shy of his fortieth birthday at Gettysburg. Lane was, like Greene, a civil engineer and had traveled widely. Before the war, he worked on mineralogical surveys in Santo Domingo, Puerto Rico and Cuba. He would be wounded at Gettysburg, but recovered with sufficient energy to participate in archaeological surveys in Palestine and the River Jordan after the war. When Lane was wounded at Gettysburg, the command of the regiment fell to twenty-three-year-old, Captain Lewis R. Stegman. Stegman would live until 1923, dying in Brooklyn.

The 137th New York and 149th New York were last in the numbering system and last to join the brigade. In many ways, the two regiments were similar—the men from both regiments were recruited from upstate New York and at about the same time. The 137th New York was organized in Binghamton, New York. The men came from the counties of Broome, Tioga, and Tompkins. Their commander at Gettysburg was Colonel David Ireland who would display great coolness under fire, holding Greene's right flank. Ireland was born in Scotland and was a tailor by trade. He was thirty-one years old at the time of the battle and would not survive the war, dying of dysentery in September 1864.

The 149th New York was organized in Syracuse, New York, from Onondaga County. Most of the men were city dwellers, living in Syracuse. They were nicknamed the "Fourth Onondaga," being the fourth regiment to be raised from that county. At Gettysburg, they were led by Colonel Henry Alanson Barnum. Barnum was a lawyer and had an interesting military career. He suffered a terrible wound at the battle of Malvern Hill that never healed properly. Later he would be awarded the Congressional Medal of Honor for his actions at Lookout Mountain. Barnum became ill during the battle of Gettysburg and command of the regiment fell to Lieutenant Colonel Charles B. Randall. Randall was born in Vermont and was a graduate of Brown University. He would be wounded on July 3, at Culp's Hill.

The 137th and 149th New York developed quite a rivalry—the men of the 137th New York were mostly country boys and did not like the city slickers of the 149th. The 137th boys referred to the 149th boys as "Salt Boilers," since the men from Binghamton, thought themselves more "aristocratic." The men of the 149th, however, eventually would get their revenge. City living had given the men from Syracuse exposure to the filth and disease often found in a city. This would help them when a typhoid fever epidemic broke out in camp. The 137th New York was hit hard, while the 149th was unaffected. The men of rural areas simply did not have the immunity of city people. The 149th watched as man after man in the ranks of the 137th was carted off in an ambulance, sick with typhoid. The 149th, therefore, referred to the 137th as the "Ambulance Brigade." Captain George K. Collins of the 149th wrote, "Mutual losses and hardships, sustained in a common cause, in the end healed all differences between the two regiments and cemented a bond of comradeship between them which will never be broken."

During the winter of 1862–1863, when the Army essentially remained idle, Greene would not let his men become complacent. He resorted to the tactics he used previously on the 60th New York. Discipline and drill became the order of the day, to the point where Greene gained a reputation for it. Still the men respected him greatly, realizing the value of their training. Greene had become a father figure to the men, treating them fairly, but with firmness. Hence, Colonel Lewis R. Stegman, of 102nd New York, said that the men referred to Greene as "Pop," their term of endearment.

The historian of Twelfth Corps, stated that, "No brigade in all the Union armies did more to enhance the military glory and renown of the Empire State." Greene's men would now follow him anywhere.

# 3

# Preparing to Fight

## The Breastworks

The men of the Second Division, Twelfth Corps, Army of the Potomac, challenged the ascent of the sun by rising early on the morning of July 2, 1863. The day would prove the bloodiest of the three at Gettysburg. By 5:00 A.M., the men were moving back in the direction of the night before, to the right of the army, toward Culp's Hill. Captain Jesse H. Jones, of the 60th New York, wrote that the division was "posted on Culp's Hill, its left forming a right angle with the right of General Wadsworth's division of the First Corps."

On the top of the larger hill, Greene's New Yorkers went into position first, to the left of the Hoosiers of the 7th, who hopefully were well rested from their midnight activities. Candy's Brigade for the moment was posted to the right rear of Greene's, and Kane's Brigade, taking up the rear of the division on the march, filed to the right of Greene. Thus, the Second Division bent back the right flank of the army, forming a right angle to the First Corps, by extending the line to cover the eastern slope of Culp's Hill.

Greene's front covered a distance of less than a quarter mile, beginning at the crest of the larger hill and following its decline toward the valley between the two hills. Its front stopped on the ridgeline of the larger hill, as Kane's men extended the line by sloping into the valley. Kane's line, thus, formed a right angle to Greene's as it descended into the valley and moved up to the crest of the lower hill. Eventually, the Twelfth Corps line would run from the crest of the larger hill, through the valley between the two hills, up the crest of the smaller hill, and follow Rock Creek to the Baltimore Pike.

Greene wrote in his Official Report that his brigade

> took position at about 6 A.M. on the right of the First Corps, on the crest of the steep and rocky hill, being thrown back nearly at right angles with the line of the First Corps, Rock Creek running past our front at the distance of 200 to 400 yards. Our position and the front were covered with a heavy growth of timber, free from undergrowth, with large ledges of rock projecting above the surface. These rocks and trees offered good cover for marksmen. The surface was very steep on our left, diminishing to a gentle slope on our right. The Second Brigade was on our right, thrown forward at a right angle to conform to the crest of the hill. On the right of this brigade was the First (Williams') Division, his right resting on an impassable mill pond on Rock Creek. As soon as we were in position, we began to intrench ourselves and throw up breastworks of the covering height, of logs, cordwood, stones, and earth. The same was done by the troops on my right.

This small portion of General Greene's report is a wealth of information, providing us with insight into his thinking, in addition to describing the activities of his men. First, he relates the position taken by his brigade, next to the First Corps, which has already been described. Then, the General gives us a lay of the land surrounding the area where his men have formed and how they can best utilize it. Next, he tells us that as soon as his men took this position, they began to "throw up breastworks." Let's examine these last two points more closely.

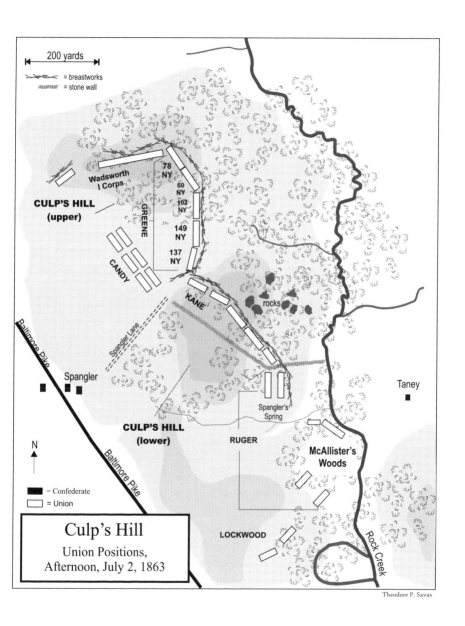

200 yards

≍≍≍ = breastworks
▓▓▓ = stone wall

Wadsworth
I Corps

78
NY

CULP'S HILL
(upper)

60
NY

GREENE

102
NY

149
NY

CANDY

137
NY

KANE

rocks

Spangler Lane

Baltimore Pike

Spangler

Taney

Spangler's
Spring

CULP'S HILL
(lower)

RUGER

N

McAllister's
Woods

= Confederate
= Union

Baltimore Pike

LOCKWOOD

Rock Creek

Culp's Hill

Union Positions,
Afternoon, July 2, 1863

Theodore P. Savas

We already know that the northern slope of the hill is the steepest. We have also established that the further one travels south, along the eastern slope of the larger hill, the lesser the grade. This area is the position that Greene's men must defend, and the general realized immediately that if the enemy was to have any chance of success, they must attack along the eastern slope. This he confirms by saying, "The surface was very steep on our left, diminishing to a gentle slope on our right." Greene was obviously not too worried about it because the hill provided cover, as he said, "for marksmen." He stipulated that the hill had "a heavy growth of timber" and the surface was covered with large rocks. However, in addition to the natural defenses furnished by the terrain, Greene included the statement that the hill was "free from undergrowth." This is an interesting point because it meant that the men had good visibility. They would be protected behind cover and afforded a clear line of sight, should the enemy attempt to storm the hill. Troops, in Civil War combat, always had a tendency to fire high. This is partly because of the trajectory of the minié ball, or bullet, when fired from a rifled musket. The minié ball would not necessarily be stable and travel along a straight line, but rather, would arch. This produced "kill zones" on the battlefield. A rifled musket sighted at 300 yards would have two "kill zones," one at about 0 to 75 yards away and the second from 250 to 350 yards. From 75 to 250 yards, the bullet would most likely rise above the head of an advancing enemy. This is why in many contemporary accounts of Civil War battles, we hear the officers exhorting their men to "aim low, boys." Nowhere would this problem of trajectory be worse than at Culp's Hill, as the men would be firing down a slope, decreasing their accuracy. It would require General Greene and his officers to lead in the trenches, keeping the men to their work.

The question of exactly who in the Twelfth Corps ordered the construction of breastworks on Culp's Hill is unknown. It may have been an immediate response, as the men gazed to their left and noticed the work of their comrades in the First Corps. We must give credit to the "Black Hat" boys of the Iron Brigade, for they were the first to entrench. However, many of the men of the Twelfth Corps mentioned the issue of who ordered them to construct breastworks. Perhaps the men remembered their previous battle at Chancellorsville and the protection that entrenchments provided. General Williams wrote, "I ordered at once a breastwork of logs to be built, having experienced their benefits at Chancellorsville."

However, there was a meeting of the officers of the Second Division upon their arrival at Culp's Hill. Captain Collins, of Greene's Brigade, recalled:

> On arriving Gen. Geary called a conference of his brigade commanders and, it was understood, submitted to them the question of building rifle-pits and expressed himself as adverse to the practice on the ground that it unfitted men for fighting without them. Gen. Greene was credited with replying that the saving of life was of far more consequence to him than any theories as to breastworks, and so far as his men were concerned, they would have them if they had time to build them. In a few minutes the officers and men were hard at work and afterwards had reason to be grateful to Gen. Greene, or somebody, for a splendid line of earthworks, without which the 3d Brigade could never have held the position of the 2d day of July against the overwhelming numbers brought against it.

Colonel Horton, in a letter written to Gettysburg historian John Bachelder, remembered:

> No orders were given to entrench but permission was given by the division commander to his brigade commanders.

Gen. Greene availed himself of this permission, and traced out a line of breastworks along his small front but Candy (1st Brigade) did not. I do not remember what Kane (2d Brigade) did at this time.

Still, Colonel Stegman of the 102nd New York related, "While thus resting an order came to build breastworks. It is said that General Geary objected to it, but General Greene persisted."

It is confirmed that the Iron Brigade was the first to build breastworks. This information, combined with the knowledge that it is unclear who in the Twelfth Corps ordered their construction (though possibly it was Greene), would support evidence that the innovation or "genius" for their use, as far as General Greene is concerned, is missing. The truth, however, is that the works constructed in Greene's front were by far the superior of the lot. Colonel Stegman also wrote:

Immediately on its arrival, by order of General Greene, who personally superintended the work, the men commenced to construct earthworks, if they may be so called, composed of logs, cordwood, stones and earth, about breast high, a good protec-

**Brigadier General John W. Geary**

tion against ordinary musketry. The works were finished by noon. The whole corps line, also Wadsworth's division, followed with works, and the right wing was ready for attack.

It may have been necessary for Greene to personally supervise the work, as some of the men were not too willing. He stated simply that the breastworks "were constructed under my immediate direction." Greene would use his training as an engineer and his penchant for rigid discipline to the fullest. Colonel Stegman, however, remembered more than that. At a speech given at the dedication of the Greene Monument at Gettysburg, he said:

> This first attempt to use earthworks having proven so futile and without benefit [at the Battle of Chancellorsville], the men of the brigade were not anxious about the works here. But they obeyed orders, particularly as General Greene walked along the lines with great care, giving personal direction as to the measurement and the angles. Many a man who sits here before me today grumbled that morning and afternoon at the persistency of "Pop Greene," their term of endearment, and prophesied that they would have their labors for their pains. Before many hours they rendered thanks and blessings for the skillful plans and judgment of their beloved commander. It seldom happened in their future career that earthworks were necessary, but the men of this brigade were never loath, after Gettysburg, to throw up all the works that might be necessary to defend any position occupied.

Captain Collins reiterated the statement of Colonel Stegman, writing:

The men grumbled a little and said it was the old trade of building works never to be used; nevertheless they brought sticks, stones, and chunks of wood, and felled trees and shoveled dirt for three or four hours.

Captain Jones gave a detailed description of how the defenses looked:

[O]ur regiment, the 60th, was on the left of the brigade. This regiment was largely composed of men accustomed to woodcraft, and they fell to work to construct log breastworks with unaccustomed heartiness. All instinctively felt that a life-and-death struggle was impending, and that every help should be used. Culp's Hill was covered with woods; so all the materials needful were at our disposal. Right and left the men felled the trees, and blocked them up into a close log fence. Piles of cordwood which lay near by were quickly appropriated. The sticks, set slanting on end against the outer face of the logs, made excellent battening. All along the rest of the line of the corps a similar defense was constructed. Fortunate regiments, which had spades and picks, strengthened their work with earth. By 10 o'clock it was finished.

The men dug trenches where they could, but in certain places the ground was solid rock, so they built up, constructing makeshift stone walls. To reinforce the trenches and the walls, the men laid down logs, from the trees they felled in their front, and piled up dirt leftover from the trenches. On top of their earthworks they placed a head log, designed to protect a soldier's head. Attaching the head log to the works created a three or four inch slit through which the men could fire. Within three to four hours the fortifications were completed. The men would

**Gettysburg Licensed Battlefield Guide Charlie Fennel points to what remains of the Union trenches on Culp's Hill. The "Military Crest" of the trenchline is clearly visible.**

commonly refer to the earthworks as the "rifle-pits" or the "pits." The earthworks are gone, but the trenchline still exists.

As important as the construction of the breastworks was, of equal value was where they were built. Greene did not place them on the top of the hill, but rather on the military crest. Charles Fennell, historian and distinguished Licensed Battlefield Guide at Gettysburg, explains:

> The military crest of a hill is the highest point where a rifleman has a clear field of fire to the base of the hill but is not, at the same time, silhouetted against the sky in the background. The military crest and not the topographic crest of a hill is the key terrain. In observing Greene's trench line on Culp's Hill, one can clearly see how that line follows the military crest of the hill affording Greene's riflemen the opportunity to place the enemy in various crossfires or interlocking fields of fire.

The "crossfires or interlocking fields of fire" that Fennell describes refers to the contour of the trench line built by the Second Division. Kane's Brigade was at a right angle to Greene's, overlooking the valley and the slope of the larger hill. Hence, if an enemy attacked Greene's front, Kane would shoot them down the flank. Not completely satisfied with his already formidable defenses, General Greene added one more thing. He built a "traverse," or a trench at a right angle at the end of his line and the beginning of Kane's. The traverse was only about the size of a company front and may have seemed superfluous at the time. It afforded protection only to troops under Greene's personal command and actually was in the rear of the Twelfth Corps line.

The ground where the traverse was built is rocky and the men could not have dug very deep, or at all, into the ground. Therefore, the traverse was probably built by piling up logs and rocks. It faced the valley, between the two hills, and the crest of the smaller hill. If the enemy gained the peak of the lower hill, the traverse would afford those units behind it cover and a clear field of fire.

Thus, Greene's men would have optimum safety while inflicting maximum punishment.

### Old Snapping Turtle

Major General George G. Meade, the commanding general of the army, arrived at Gettysburg at about midnight, after the fighting of the first day had ceased. It had been a wicked ride from Taneytown, Maryland, the general and his retinue moving as rapidly as possible to the field. He arrived at Cemetery Hill in the darkness and began a personal reconnaissance of the field. By the time the sun was coming up, Meade, who probably did not sleep at all that night, made his way toward Culp's Hill. At some point on his ride he met and spoke with General Slocum. Meade then ordered Brigadier General Henry J. Hunt to move some artillery to the right, to cover a gap in the Union line. From that point, as the sun was rising, Meade would

**Major General
George G. Meade**

become almost obsessed with the condition of his right flank. He expected an early morning attack against this flank, but it never came. If the Rebels would not throw the first punch this day, then Meade would. He began to plan an offensive, on his right, attacking the Confederate left. The Twelfth Corps, with the Fifth Corps nearby, would lead the attack and the Sixth Corps, which was marching to the field, could be used as a reserve.

Colonel Fox, historian of the Twelfth Corps, wrote:

> General Meade, after examining a part of the field on the morning of the second, decided to take the offensive. He issued an order at nine-thirty A.M., directing General Slocum, who was in command of the Twelfth and Fifth Corps, to make arrangements to move forward with these troops and attack the enemy on his front.

Slocum, however, had thoroughly examined the terrain on the right and advised Meade against making an attack. The rocky, broken ground, heavily wooded and hilly, was not conducive for offensive operations. Colonel Fox stated,

"General Warren, the chief engineer of the army, concurred. The movement was abandoned." Meade instructed the Fifth Corps to move to the left and the "Sixth to occupy its place as a reserve for the right."

Although underexamined, Meade's abandoned proposal of an offensive on the right had massive repercussions. General Slocum, because of the "Pipe Creek Circular," seemed to believe that he was the commander of a fictitious right wing. The "Pipe Creek Circular" was a contingency plan created by Meade, which was never implemented because the clash of arms at Gettysburg made it irrelevant. It directed that if the Confederate army assumed the offensive and attacked, the Army of the Potomac would fall back to a defensive line and hold Lee in check, if necessary, to northern Maryland at Pipe Creek. The circular stated, upon implementation, that Slocum would assume command of a newly designated "right wing," to include the Fifth Corps, in addition to his own. Meade's offensive plans, which would have placed the Fifth Corps under Slocum, probably

**Major General
Henry W. Slocum**

reinforced his thinking that the circular was still in effect. It was, of course, totally obsolete, but not in Slocum's mind. As a result, he created a convoluted chain of command for the Twelfth Corps. If he was the right-wing commander, then General Alpheus Williams, normally leading the First Division, was now the Twelfth Corps commander, thus replacing Slocum. Then Williams would be replaced, and the man replacing Williams would have to be replaced, and so on, and so on. This confusion would plague the corps through the entire battle.

Meade's seeming preoccupation with his right flank caused him to overlook his left. Consequently, Major General Daniel E. Sickles would disobey orders and move his Third Corps about three quarters of a mile forward, isolating himself from the rest of the army. The result was the now infamous "Sickles Salient." Sickles would also accuse Meade of not wanting to fight at Gettysburg, using the "Pipe Creek Circular" as evidence in his arguments. Meade, of course, was a good soldier, if not a great one, but he has never gotten the respect that he deserves. His plans to attack Lee on the morning of the second day prove, without question, his desire to fight. All this, of course, is another story.

Charles Fennell brings up another interesting theory concerning Meade's abandoned plans. He writes:

> [T]he fact that his trusted subordinates had pronounced the ground on the Union right unfit for offensive operations may have contributed to his decision later in the day to remove the entire Twelfth Corps from the Culp's Hill area.

We can see Meade, at mid-morning, careworn, haggard from lack of sleep and as always, nervous. One of Meade's staff members described him as a:

> thorough soldier, and a mighty clear-headed man; and one who does not move unless he knows where

and how many his men are; where and how many his enemy's men are; and what sort of country he had to go through. I never saw a man in my life who was so characterized by straightforward truthfulness as he is. He will pitch into himself in a moment, if he thinks he had done wrong; and woe to those, no matter who they are, who do not do it right!

Meade was brutally honest, which was his best trait; his worst was his temper, which sometimes got the better of him. When he became angry, it was said his eyes would bulge out and he looked like an "old snapping turtle."

### "Old Clubby"

After waking on their arms in the dark, Confederate soldiers of Major General Edward Johnson's Division, Second Corps, Army of Northern Virginia, prepared for battle. They expected to be fighting as the sun appeared; after all, that was the plan of General Lee, to attack at daybreak. But nothing happened. In fact, Lee informed Ewell that the step-off time of the assault had to be pushed back to 9:00 A.M. So, the men waited and waited, until finally the time of the attack was scheduled for 4:00 P.M.

Lee wanted to strike the Federals early before they had time to fully prepare their defenses and new troops arrived. He knew that to maintain the initiative he had to attack, but time was favoring his opponent. On the offense, planning takes time. Moving large bodies of troops into position to execute the plan takes enormous amounts of time. Lee had no more time, but Meade had all the time in the world, and he was digging in.

Lee's strategy of attack, against what was now a "fishhook" battle line, had not changed from the previous night's meeting with the officers of the Second Corps. Longstreet would lead the main assault, striking the Union left, while Ewell made a diversionary attack against the right. Longstreet's blow would deliver the knockout, while

Ewell's feint would pin the Federals down, eliminating their ability to quickly reinforce the threatened flank. But Longstreet was stalling, due to miscommunication or other reasons, and the plan was momentarily stymied.

As the hours passed, Lee asked Ewell again if he could not strike the Federal right, as the main Confederate assault. Lee and Ewell personally examined the position together in the daylight, and it was agreed that the chance of success was dismal. Everyone would have to wait for Longstreet.

The already high level of anxiety running through Ewell's veins assuredly increased with the news of the captured courier the previous evening. The real possibility of the Union Fifth Corps marching into his left flank and rear, along the Hanover Road, was alarming. The famous "Stonewall Brigade," part of Johnson's Division, was dispatched to Brinkerhoff's Ridge on the Hanover Road to guard against this movement and to protect the flank. The 2nd Virginia, part of that famed brigade, would be tasked with the greater part of this duty.

The incessant "popping" of the skirmishers kept the battlefield far from silent in this area, even though no major fighting was taking place. While the majority of Johnson's men sat broiling to a crisp in the scorching sun, waiting to attack, the Stonewall Brigade was kept very busy. Throughout the day and into the evening, they traded shots with various units of the Army of the Potomac, holding down the flank. The fighting at Brinkerhoff's Ridge would center on the possession of a stone wall, and though seemingly unimportant, its ramifications regarding the outcome of the fight at Culp's Hill, and subsequently the entire battle, were decisive.

Though the action at Brinkerhoff's Ridge on July 2 could probably produce another small book, and deservedly so, the surface of it will be only lightly touched upon here.

Men from Williams's Division of the Twelfth Corps, who had assembled near the ridge the previous day in their abortive assault, were the first to confront the Virginians. Later, the 9th Massachusetts, known as the "Irish Ninth," would square off with the Stonewall Brigade, in this dangerous but necessary game of death. Colonel Patrick R. Guiney, who was born in Tipperary, Ireland, and would later lose an eye in the war, commanded the Bay State men. While the 9th Massachusetts exchanged unpleasantness with their foe, the Fifth Corps was diverted by Meade from the Hanover Road to the Union's main battle line. This placed the 9th Massachusetts alone against the Confederate left flank. Soon, however, two Union cavalry brigades arrived under the command of Brigadier General David McM. Gregg. But to Colonel Guiney's amazement the cavalry offered him no support. He complained his men were nothing more than bodyguards, as the horsemen rested in his regiment's rear. Rest, however, was not something that soldiers at Gettysburg could easily obtain, as the Union cavalry troopers were called upon to relieve the 9th Massachusetts.

The hour had reached 3:00 P.M. as part of the 10th New York Cavalry, stationed at Gettysburg earlier in the war, moved into position. Johnson was now beginning his preparations for the advance to Culp's Hill and could not leave this threat on his left flank. The Stonewall Brigade was ordered to shift left along Hanover Road to counter the hazard presented by the pesky cavalry. The 2nd Virginia, commanded by Colonel John Nadenbousch, now north of the road after the brigade's movement, was directed to

> clear the field, and advance into the wood, and ascertain, if possible, what force the enemy had at that point, which he did at a single dash, his men advancing with great spirit, driving the enemy's skirmishers out of the clear ground and following them into the woods.

The Virginians proceeded to advance, as the 10th New York pushed fresh companies into the fray. As the fighting continued, the New Yorkers were relieved by elements of the 3rd Pennsylvania, 1st New Jersey, and Purnell Legion (Maryland). Both sides would realize that the domination of Brinkerhoff's Ridge would depend on the control of a "stone fence" running along its crest. A footrace will ensue and the 3rd Pennsylvania will outrun the Virginians, reaching the fence just twenty paces ahead. Aided by Captain William Rank's section of the 3rd Pennsylvania Heavy Artillery, the cavalrymen will drive back the Rebels, but momentarily. Colonel Nadenbousch will counterattack, in the darkness, gaining a portion of the wall briefly, before being driven back a second time. The casualties on both sides were minor—the Union side had four killed and nine wounded. The 2nd Virginia had six men either wounded or captured. With darkness covering the field, both sides quieted down.

As General Johnson was making his preparations to advance, Colonel Nadenbousch "reported that the enemy had a large force of cavalry (supposed to be two brigades), two regiments of infantry, and a battery of artillery." This information was incorrect, but required attention. Brigadier General James A. Walker, commander of the Stonewall Brigade, recounted the next events:

> This information I communicated through a staff officer to Major General Johnson, and immediately thereafter received information from Major (H. K.) Douglas, of his staff, that the line was about to advance, with instructions from General Johnson to remain on the flank, if I thought it necessary.
>
> As our flank and rear would have been entirely uncovered and unprotected in the event of my moving with the rest of the division, and as our movement must have been made in full view of the

enemy, I deemed it prudent to hold my position until after dark, which I did.

An interesting caveat concerning the fighting at Brinkerhoff's Ridge, provided by National Park Historian Paul Shevchuk, involved Brigadier General Albert Jenkins. Jenkins and his rowdy group of horsemen arrived at Gettysburg on the night of July 1 just as the fighting was dying down and thus did not participate in the action. Jenkins's men made camp spread out along the Harrisburg Road, where previously Early had launched his attack. The following morning Jenkins was summoned to meet with General Lee at the commander's headquarters. The discussion between the two soldiers was not documented, but it seems clear that Jenkins was ordered to support Ewell in his theatre of operations, on the Confederate left flank. Shevchuk writes:

> Jenkins' task in the grand scheme of things was simple. His brigade of 1,300 men was to ride to Johnson's extreme left flank and relieve Smith and Gordon of the burden of watching for the enemy. Once this had been accomplished, Ewell would have all his brigades available for the grand assault upon the Union line.

Jenkins, who anticipated an early morning attack and, evidently, never received information regarding the delay of Longstreet's Corps, never made it to Ewell's left. After gathering up his men, the brigade began to ride toward the flank, but halted about mid-morning by Rock Creek, a short distance beyond Blocher's (now called Barlow's) Knoll. The reason for this stop is uncertain. Jenkins then turned around with his staff and rode to the crest of Blocher's Knoll and began to examine the Union artillery positions on Cemetery Hill and Culp's Hill. Jenkins dismounted, held the reins of his horse in one hand, and with the other looked through his field glasses. Soon, a courier appeared who was from Jenkins's staff, but was temporarily assigned to Major General Rodes. The courier had orders from Ewell, for Jenkins, instructing him exactly where to deploy his brigade. The courier traced the position for Jenkins on a map; the area was Johnson's left flank. A series of cannon shots now erupted from Cemetery Hill, aimed for the group of officers on the knoll. After a few close calls, one of the shells exploded amongst the officers and Jenkins horse was killed. More unfortunate, General Jenkins was lying injured on the ground, his head and face covered in blood. Jenkins would survive his wound, but Jeb Stuart took his brigade with him, depriving Ewell of its use. Thus, Johnson was forced to commit the Stonewall Brigade to guard his flank, leaving him minus a brigade in the attack on Culp's Hill.

Major General Edward Johnson was a colorful, robust man, forty-seven years of age, and despite his afflictions led his division of four brigades with a battle strength of 6,433 at Gettysburg. He was born in Salisbury, Virginia, in Chesterfield County, but his parents moved to Kentucky when he was still a child. He attended West Point and

**Major General
Edward Johnson**

graduated in the class of 1838. He fought the Seminoles in Florida, saw service in the Mexican War, and participated in the Utah Expedition. He resigned from the U.S. Army on June 10, 1861 and became colonel of the 12th Georgia Infantry. He was promoted to brigadier general that same year and in 1862 he commanded the "Army of the Northwest," which was about the size of a brigade. He led his small army, with distinction, in Stonewall Jackson's Valley campaign in 1862. At the Battle of McDowell in May that same year, Johnson suffered a serious wound in his ankle. This injury would require him to walk with a cane that many thought resembled a fence rail. He also suffered an affliction in one eye, causing him to wink uncontrollably. A soldier in the Stonewall Brigade wrote of Johnson:

> He was wounded in the foot. He very seldom carried a sword, but nearly always a big hickory club, or cane. We always called him "Old Clubby Johnson," to distinguish him from the other Johnsons.

A soldier in the 2nd Louisiana Infantry, during the Battle of Winchester, wrote this account of Johnson:

> During this engagement Major General Edward Johnson was seen riding in front of the line with a large hickory club. He was called by the boys "Club" Johnson. Earlier in the war, while in the Valley, he was called "Alleghany Ned."

Johnson was evidently fearless around the ladies, as well as in battle, as his activities in Richmond during his recuperation from his wound caused quite a bit of gossip. Douglas Southall Freeman, borrowing a quote from Mary Chestnut, wrote in his classic study of the Army of Northern Virginia, "Lee's Lieutenants":

The fashionable ladies may laugh at Edward
Johnson's social oddities and may say that his head
is in three tiers, like the papal tiara, but after he
receives a Division and leads it in battle, no soldier
ever laughs at "Old Allegheny." Johnson does well
in nearly all his fights, hits hard and wins the confi-
dence of his men.

A story of him in battle goes:

The Federal soldiers knew General Johnson by
sight, and, during the battle one time, being separated a little from his command, some of them hal-
looed out: "There's old Johnson; let's flank him!"
Johnson heard them, and, waving his club in the air,
exclaimed: "Yes, damn you, flank me if you can."

At the Battle of Spotsylvania, in May 1864, Johnson's
command defended the "Bloody Angle" and Johnson was
seen "swinging his cane at the bluecoats swarming over
the breastworks." He was later captured, with most of his
command, but was exchanged. He then went on to lead a
division in the Tennessee campaign in General Stephen D.
Lee's Corps and was subsequently captured, this time at
the battle of Nashville. He was released in July 1865 and
went home to Chesterfield County to be a farmer. He died
in 1873 in Richmond his body lay in state at the Capitol.
Johnson was one tough customer.

Brigadier General John M. Jones commanded an all-
Virginia brigade in Johnson's Division. He was born in
Charlottesville, Virginia, in 1820 and graduated from West
Point in the class of 1841, the same year as Major General
John F. Reynolds. He is often confused with Confederate
General John R. Jones. After the battle of Chancellorsville,
Lieutenant Colonel John M. Jones, who was serving in the
capacity of Inspector General in Jubal Early's division, had

**Brigadier General
John M. Jones**

the opportunity for promotion and an appointment to command a brigade. Freeman wrote that it

> was suggested vaguely in Lee's letter to Davis at the time of the appointment: "Should (Jones) fail in his duty, he will instantly resign." If this meant that Jones's enemy was strong drink, the new Brigadier met and over came that adversary.

Evidently, Jones had a drinking problem and made some sort of promise to Lee to abstain from alcohol. As Freeman suggests, Jones did not drink, at least, not that anyone knew of, for he commanded his brigade until he was killed in the Battle of the Wilderness in 1864. The regiments in Jones's brigade at Gettysburg consisted of the 21st, 25th, 42nd, 44th, 48th, and 50th Virginia Infantry.

Another brigade in Johnson's division was that of Brigadier General Francis Nicholls and was comprised of men from the land of the French Quarter, gumbo, and strange politics, otherwise known as the state of Louisiana. So strange was the state's politics that General Nicholls, who lost his left arm in 1862 and had his left foot blown off by a shell at Chancellorsville, ran for governor of the state in 1876. His campaign motto was "Vote for what's left of General Nicholls." The outcome of the election was as bizarre as Nicholls's motto, for he did not win, but he also did not lose. He ran as a democrat and refused to accept his republican opponent's apparent victory, so the state was run in a dual administration until Nicholls was recognized as the winner by Federal authorities.

At any rate, Nicholls did not serve at Gettysburg and his brigade was commanded by Colonel Jesse M. Williams. Williams was from Mansfield, Louisiana, and attended the University of Alabama. He served in the 2nd Louisiana Infantry taking command of that regiment in 1862. He fought in most of the Army of Northern Virginia's major battles. When Nicholls had his foot blown off, Williams took command of the brigade. He would ultimately relinquish his leadership of the brigade after Gettysburg and return to his former post with the 2nd Louisiana. The regiments in this all-Louisiana brigade consisted of the 1st, 2nd, 10th, 14th, and 15th Infantries.

The famed Stonewall Brigade, not a participant in the attack but nonetheless part of Johnson's Division, was commanded by Brigadier General James A. Walker. The Stonewall Brigade earned its title, like its namesake, General Thomas Stonewall Jackson, at the battle of First Manassas. It became the most popular and storied of all Confederate brigades in the war, so much so that the Confederate government allowed its nickname to be its officially accepted title. It was the only Confederate brigade in the war to be so honored. Historian James I. Robertson, Jr., who wrote a history of the brigade, said, "the brigade achieved a reputation almost without parallel for agility, gallantry, and pugnacity." Their delay, however, in reaching the scene of the action at Culp's Hill, will be critical. General Walker was not very well liked by the soldiers in the brigade, at least initially when he took command, because he was not one of them. He was the type that kept to himself mostly, but enjoyed, as Robertson writes, "a good-sized drink, liked to play practical jokes, and enjoyed life in general, especially if a fight of some kind seemed likely." He was, of course, a Virginian, and attended the Virginia Military Institute, where he was court-martialed in his senior year. It seems the young Walker got into a heated argument with Professor Thomas Jackson, the future "Stonewall." When Jackson shouted down the cadet, Walker felt insulted and challenged him to a duel. Jackson declined the duel and instead, initiated court-martial proceedings. However, later, during the war, Walker got along fine with Jackson. After a month or so commanding the Stonewall Brigade, most of the soldiers began to accept him and he was nick-named "Stonewall Jim." The regiments in the renowned Stonewall Brigade consisted of the 2nd, 4th, 5th, 27th, and 33rd Virginia Infantries.

**Brigadier General
James A. Walker**

**Brigadier General
George H. Steuart**

The last brigade in the division was a conglomeration of regiments from three different states and was led by Brigadier General George H. "Maryland" Steuart. He was nicknamed "Maryland" so as not to be confused with the more famous Jeb Stuart. "Maryland" Steuart was from Baltimore and was a month or so short of his thirty-fifth birthday at Gettysburg. He graduated from West Point in 1848 when he was only nineteen years old, but finished thirty-seventh out of a class of thirty-eight. He became a member of the 2nd Dragoons and later, the 2nd U.S. Cavalry, serving on the frontier. In 1861, upon joining the Confederate service, he became a captain in the cavalry and then eventually colonel of the 1st Maryland Infantry. In March 1862, he took command over a brigade of four Virginia regiments, which included the 1st Maryland. He was seriously wounded in the battle of Cross Keys in the Valley campaign, but recovered in time to command at Gettysburg. His brigade consisted of the 10th, 23rd, and 37th Virginia, 1st and 3rd North Carolina, and the 1st Maryland Battalion.

These were the men that "Old Clubby" Johnson would lead to Culp's Hill.

# 4

# THE ARTILLERY FIGHT

BEFORE THE BATTLE, Cemetery Hill served as a burial ground for the citizenry of the local area, with Evergreen Cemetery, as it was called, crowning its heights. After the battle, a new plot, the Soldier's National Cemetery, was added "as a final resting place" for the soldiers killed at Gettysburg. The hill, consequently, has had a somewhat dual existence. Today, it serves as a reminder to all Americans that the cost of freedom is sometimes paid, as President Lincoln said, "with the last full measure of devotion." The Soldier's National Cemetery provides everlasting proof of the desperate struggle waged on the fields in and around the sleepy little town. There is no other piece of property in America, save possibly Arlington National Cemetery and the World Trade Centers in New York City, that is so sacred.

Cemetery Hill also reminds the visitor that the great battle was fought directly on its environs. It served as an artillery position for the Union army, while the dead already lay there. In fact, it was a massive artillery position, easily recognized today by the existence of the guns that mark the site, but rest silently, as a monument to the colossal events of the time.

Traditionally, students of the battle reference the hill in sections, referring to the portion of it east of the Baltimore Pike as East Cemetery Hill. The Union guns positioned on this side of the hill were under the command of Colonel

**Colonel
Charles S. Wainwright**

Charles Shiels Wainwright. Wainwright hailed from the Hudson valley in upstate New York, where his father owned a farm known as "The Meadows." The family was quite wealthy from selling the farm's produce in the markets in New York City. Wainwright, due to his father's influence, did not join the Union army immediately at the onset of the war. It was not until the fall of 1861 that Wainwright, with the help of political connections, became a major with the 1st New York Artillery. He later was promoted to commander of the First Corps Artillery, Army of the Potomac. Wainwright also kept a daily journal that is a classic of Civil War literature. At Gettysburg, he was in charge of batteries from his own corps and also some from the Eleventh Corps.

A battery, in Civil War terms, was a grouping of six guns in the Union and could range anywhere from four to six guns for the Confederacy. All the guns in a Union battery at Gettysburg were of the same type, but Confederates batteries often contained a mixture of different types. Each two guns in a battery were called a "section." There were basically two types of guns in the Civil War, rifles and smoothbores. Rifled guns were the new technology of the time. Inside the barrel of the gun, or its bore, were spiraling grooves that ran the length of the tube. The rifling in cannons, which worked the same in muskets, helped to stabilize the projectile and caused it to spin. The spinning motion increased the speed of the projectile, or shell, and also gave it much greater range and accuracy. Rifled guns proved to be excellent in battery against battery fire, or gun versus gun. This technology, however, was not preferred by most Civil War artillerists. They liked the old-fashioned smoothbore, or Napoleon (named after Napoleon III), because it was extremely effective as an antipersonnel weapon. It fired a solid, round cannon ball, as opposed to the rifled shell, which was conical or otherwise looked like a large, modern-day bullet. The solid cannon ball weighed twelve pounds and was aimed slightly short of the advancing infantry. If the ground was hard enough, the ball bounced and proceeded to go "bowling for heads," annihilating any object that was unfortunate enough to get in its path. The Napoleon was also extremely effective at firing canister, or what looked like a large coffee can made of paper or canvas, filled with little iron balls. Canister, to put it mildly, was lethal. Often artillerists would load their "pieces" with double rounds of canister and turn a perfectly green field into a horror scene, with twitching and mangled bodies piled on top of one another.

The three most prominent models of guns were the Napoleon, the three-inch Ordnance rifle, and the ten-pounder Parrott. The Parrott, named after its inventor, James Parrott, was very similar to the Ordnance rifle, except that the Parrott had a cast-iron tube, reinforced at the breech by a wrought-iron hoop. Rifled guns had tremendous range, but Civil War artillerists used "direct fire," only firing at what they could see. Therefore, they almost never fired at a target more than a mile and a quarter distant.

Limbers and caissons, which were called wagons, though they were more like horse-drawn carts, carried ammunition chests, tools, and equipment for the guns. Each gun in a battery was assigned two limbers and a caisson. Normally, one limber, with the horses facing the enemy, was placed six yards in back of the gun during the action. The second limber, with the caisson, would be eleven yards in the rear of the first limber. Jack Coggins, in his terrific book, *Arms & Equipment of the Civil War,* describes the frontage of a Civil War battery in battle:

> In the field, spacing depended both on the tactical situation and the lay of the land. Regulations called for 14-yard intervals between pieces. Allowing 2 yards per piece, battery front was 82 yards.

It took nine men to operate one gun, including the chief-of-section and chief-of-piece. The chief-of-section, usually a lieutenant, was in charge of two guns and the chief-of-piece, or gunnery sergeant, commanded one gun. The other gunners in the crew were referred to by numbers, one through seven respectively, each with his own job. The six horses that pulled the gun and the limber (also six horses followed, pulling a limber and a caisson) were divided into teams of two. The front team was called the lead pair, the middle team the swing pair, and the final two the wheel pair.

Regulations are handy texts of rules, but by this time in the war, especially during this artillery fight, soldiers on either side had difficulty following the regulations for artillery.

Colonel Wainwright had thirteen three-inch Ordnance rifles and six Napoleons under his immediate supervision, pointing at the Rebel batteries beyond. The six Napoleons were under the management of Captain

Greenleaf T. Stevens, the 5th Maine battery, and they were posted on the western slope of Culp's Hill, which connected the rise to East Cemetery Hill. Today, the area is named "Stevens Knoll" after the captain. Wainwright's colleague, Major Thomas Osborn, commander of the Eleventh Corps Artillery, was in charge of managing the guns on West Cemetery Hill. He had over forty guns under his immediate control, yet only ten were aimed at the Confederate batteries poised to cover the attack at Culp's Hill. All of these ten guns were rifled. Five guns of the Twelfth Corps will also participate in the fight, firing from Culp's Hill.

Major Osborn was born in New Jersey, but his family moved near to Watertown, New York when he was a child. Osborn studied law at Watertown, and as Harry Pfanz writes, "had no interest in military matters—in fact, he found the idea of military service repulsive."

Wainwright's and Osborn's antagonist was Major Joseph White Latimer, from Prince William County, Virginia. Latimer, known as the "Boy Major," was born on August 27, 1843, making him under twenty years of age at Gettysburg. Latimer had taken command of the artillery of Johnson's

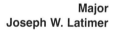

**Major
Joseph W. Latimer**

Division when Lieutenant Colonel R. Snowden Andrews, as Latimer wrote, "was struck in the arm by a shot from a lingering sharpshooter, which gave him a severe, but not serious, flesh wound" at the battle of Winchester on the march north. Latimer, despite his young age, was well loved and respected by the men, Ewell even referred to him as the "Young Napoleon." Douglas Southall Freeman wrote of him, "those who knew the younger artillerists ranked Latimer with Pegram and with Pelham."

Latimer arrived in the darkness with the division after the first day's fighting and placed his guns in the safety of a wheat field east of town. As the sun began to rise, he searched for a location where his guns could be used for maximum effect. Unfortunately, no such site existed and Latimer was forced to settle for a spot where his guns could simply participate. The area he chose was Benner's Hill, a hundred feet above Rock Creek, which ran just under a halfmile in length in a north–south direction and was bisected by the Hanover Road. The hill was bald, lacking any kind of cover, and thus Latimer's guns would be out in the open. A more famous Confederate artillerist at Gettysburg, Colonel E. P. Alexander, said of Latimer's position that it

> was but a single position where the confederates could plant guns to fire upon this line, and that [it was] an inferior one, giving little shelter and exposed to an enfilade fire. It was so contracted that with difficulty 14 guns were crowded upon it, within about a 1000 yards of the enemy. It might have been foreseen that this battery, exposed to the fire of double its number of guns, would soon be put out of action.

It may have seemed so for Alexander and Latimer, but before the contest began, Colonel Wainwright recorded in his journal:

> The rebel guns had the advantage of us. They were
> on higher ground, and having plenty of room were
> able to place their guns some thirty yards apart,
> while ours were not over twelve; and the two faces
> of our line meeting here, the limbers stood
> absolutely crowded together.

Perhaps this is a case of a soldier making more out of his victory than actually was the case, or maybe Wainwright really believed he was disadvantaged. Every other source, however, agrees that the Confederate guns on Benner's Hill were in a very inferior position. Latimer must have thought so, because he kept his guns under cover until the time of the attack. Prior to the placement of his guns, General Johnson asked Major W. W. Goldsborough of the 1st Maryland Battalion of Infantry for his opinion of Benner's Hill as an artillery position. Goldsborough rode to the crest of Benner's Hill and quickly noticed that the Union gunners on Cemetery Hill would easily dominate any guns placed there. Goldsborough was certain that Johnson would not allow Latimer to post his guns on the hill as soon as he reported his findings. To Goldsborough's horror, however, Johnson appeared with his staff and gave an order to have Latimer occupy the hill. Goldsborough was mortified, realizing that many a good boy from his home state would probably meet their fate at Benner's Hill.

Latimer had a total of twenty guns at his disposal, the fourteen mentioned by Alexander and six longer ranged pieces, twenty-pounder Parrott rifles. Four of these twenty-pounders belonged to the Rockbridge Artillery, from that county in the Shenandoah Valley of Virginia. Being of the religious sort, the men in the battery nicknamed their four pieces Matthew, Mark, Luke, and John. Today, these guns of the gospel are located on the campus of the Virginia Military Institute, where Latimer studied his profession under Stonewall Jackson. Latimer was not entirely alone, as approximately forty guns from A. P. Hill's Third Corps, along

Seminary Ridge, faced the Union batteries on Cemetery Hill. Thus the Union artillery would be firing from three positions—Cemetery Hill, Stevens Knoll, and Culp's Hill—and the Confederates from Seminary Ridge and Benner's Hill.

As Longstreet began the main assault at 4:00 P.M., General Johnson ordered Latimer to post his guns and begin firing. In accordance with General Lee's plan, Ewell was executing his "demonstration" against the Union right. Latimer placed his fourteen guns to the left, or south of the Hanover Road and put the heavier twenty-pounders to the right, or north of the road, positioning them slightly to the rear of his main line. The guns soon began to open, with the Union gunners responding in kind and all hell broke loose.

Shells of all kinds began to fall and explode everywhere around the Rebels. Balls of iron struck the ground and bounced, seeking to smash a gun, a horse, or someone's head. The ground seemed to implode from beneath as iron projectiles smacked the surface, tearing up the land without impunity. It seemed that scarcely any living thing could survive, and many did not. Not even the sparse amount of trees were safe, as round shot cracked through the branches, sending splinters in the air. Horses were killed while restrained in their harnesses, and others around them, filled with fright, tried to run while confined. Men were wounded and killed and their comrades ignored them, in the heat of battle, keeping to their work of death. And the guns continued to spew with rapidity. Lieutenant Randolph McKim said, while in the rear of the hill with the infantry, he counted 180 discharges in a minute. He stated, "It was a beautiful sight, but an awful one."

Captain William D. Brown, commander of the Chesapeake Artillery of Maryland, rode to the front of his men as the shooting started and asked his men

> for the honor of our native State, to stand manfully to our guns. The words were still upon his lips when he fell, dreadfully mangled by a solid shot.

Three guns of the Chesapeake battery would be taken out of commission, silenced by the aim of the Federal guns. With tears in his eyes, Sergeant Crowley of the battery stood silent around the wreckage. Another member of the Chesapeake Artillery approached him and recorded what he witnessed:

> Approaching the veteran he pointed, with a trembling voice, to his dead and wounded comrades. There were Doctor Jack Brian, and Daniel Dougherty, and brave little Cusick. They belonged to his detachment. And even while he was deploring their loss, a solid shot struck Thaddeus Parker and literally disemboweled him and killed the two lead horses he was holding.

Billy Yank fared no better, Wainwright remarking that "their fire was the most accurate I have ever seen on the part of their artillery, and the distance was just right, say 1,400 yards." He was sitting with General Ames of the Eleventh Corps, on a stone wall between some of his guns, as the skies erupted. The twenty-pounder guns of the gospel, possibly, preached a parable that Wainwright could not forget. No more than ten yards from where he sat, "two instances of the destruction which can be caused by a single twenty-pounder shot" occurred. He described the scene:

> One of these shot struck in the centre of a line of infantry who were lying down behind the wall. Taking the line lengthways, it literally ploughed up two or three yards of men, killing and wounding a dozen or more. Fortunately it did not burst, for it struck so near where we were sitting that it covered us with dust.
>
> The other was a shell which burst directly under Cooper's left gun, killed one man outright, blew

another all to pieces, so that he died in half an hour, and wounded the other three.

Colonel Wainwright was speaking of Battery B, 1st Pennsylvania Light Artillery, commanded by Captain James H. Cooper. Cooper, in one of his first shots, scored a direct hit on a Confederate caisson, causing a terrific explosion. Captain James Stewart, whose battery was nearby, ordered his men to give three cheers for the Pennsylvania gunners.

> The echo had scarcely died away when one of my caissons met the same fate. Then the hurrah was on the side of the Johnnies. It was the cleanest job I ever saw. The three chests were sent skyward and the horses started off on a run toward the town, but one of the swing team got over the traces, throwing him down and causing the rest of the team to halt.

Stewart's men chased after them and upon bringing them back, Stewart noticed "every hair was burnt off the tails and manes of the wheel horses." Stewart inquired as to where the wheel driver was, as he had not returned with the group. A man reported that he saw him heading for a nearby spring and Stewart sent the man to look for him. All the excitement was not over for Stewart, however.

> A few minutes after, one of my limbers was also blown up, causing a loss of two men and two horses. While looking at the limber, a man came to me with a piece of jacket in his hand, and said: "Sir, this is all I can find of Smith, the driver." About a month after I received a communication from a surgeon in charge of the Cass Hospital, Detroit City, that Smith was a patient there and had entirely lost his sight.

**Painting by William H. Shelton, titled "The Runaway Limber,"
which depicts the action on Cemetery Hill.**

Colonel Wainwright said that he "had two pretty narrow escapes myself, one the closest I have ever had." He thought the two instances indicated that he had become "indifferent" to shells flying and bursting all around him, even thinking them "harmless," as he became accustomed to the combat. He admitted that both cases were, therefore, a "result of carelessness." The first close call came when a shell struck about six yards in front of him, "burying itself deep in the ground almost under my feet." He wondered if it would explode upward, which would probably kill him, or "if it would drive out by the hole it entered when it burst." It did just that and Wainwright survived. The second case seemed extremely thoughtless, as Wainwright walked in front of a gun about to fire. He forgot that one of the guns in battery was a little in the rear of the others, and he "passed to the front of it just at that instant it was fired." He realized that if he had taken one more step forward, "they would have blown their colonel as far as ever the British blew mutinous Sepoys. The flash fairly burnt my face; a sudden stop, an exclamation of 'close shave,' and I went on."

On the Confederate side, most of Johnson's infantry were behind Benner's Hill, along the Hanover Road, and shots fired long by the Union guns fell amongst them. Shells crashed and exploded around them, yet Lieutenant McKim found time to hold religious services, first with the 10th Virginia and later with 1st Maryland Battalion. He wrote, "There was a peculiar solemnity in thus appealing to the Almighty for His protection on the battle field itself, just before rushing forward to assault the lines of the enemy." The men of Brigadier General John M. Jones's brigade had no such opportunity for worship, as they were sent forward to support the artillery. Jones moved his men to the south slope of Benner's Hill, to the left of Latimer's guns. There he halted his men "under cover of a range of low hills, about 300 yards in rear and to the left of the battalion of artillery." As Lieutenant Colonel L. H. N. Sayler of the 50th Virginia moved his regiment with the brigade, he quickly realized that his comrades by the guns were becoming overwhelmed. He said, "they could not long continue the contest; however, Major Latimer held his ground till several of his pieces had been silenced by the loss of gunners." The 50th Virginia, as infantrymen often did, went to the aid of the cannoneers, working the guns. While in this role the regiment suffered a man killed and two wounded.

The barrage of deadly missiles did not discriminate between friend and foe, as Colonel Wainwright could attest. Yankee infantry at the base of East Cemetery Hill found that the fire of their artillery could be just as deadly as that posed by the Rebels. Colonel Orlando Smith wrote that his men

> were constantly exposed, not only to the fire in front, but to the shot and shell coming from the bat-

teries placed opposite the Twelfth Corps, on the right. Moreover, some casualties were occasioned by the premature explosion of some of the shells from our own batteries. Though the situation was at times of the most trying character, never a man faltered, to my knowledge, or complained, but every man seemed inspired by a determination to hold his position, dead or alive.

The men of 55th Ohio experienced the brunt of one of the most incredible shots in the entire Civil War. One shot was said to have killed and wounded twenty-seven men!

Aside from such remarkable shooting, the artillerists suffered the worst, especially on the Confederate side. Like Colonel Salyer mentioned, the contest was rapidly favoring the Union boys. The Federal artillery quickly bore down, got their ranges fixed, and poured lethal punishment upon the Southerners. The cannons on Cemetery Hill were soon aided by guns of the Twelfth Corps, which fired down the Confederate left flank from Culp's Hill. Lieutenant Edward D. Muhlenberg described the action:

The density of the growth of timber, the irregularity and extremely broken character of the ground, studded with immense bowlders, prevented the artillery from taking position in the line proper of the corps. It was, therefore, held in reserve and readiness to answer all calls which might be made upon it by the future movements of the opposing forces. The enemy seriously annoying the left of the line of the Twelfth, a vacant space eligible for a battery was found about 200 yards on the right of the First Corps. At 3:30 P.M. one gun (10-pounder Parrott), and at 5 P.M. two more of the same caliber, Knap's Independent Pennsylvania, the three under charge of Lieutenant Geary, were placed in position, and were joined by one section of 12-pounder

Napoleons (K, Fifth U.S. Artillery), under charge of Second Lieut. William E. Van Reed. The moment their presence was observed, the enemy opened with eight guns; continued an incessant fire for some thirty minutes; then, having a caisson exploded, ceased.

It would have been extremely difficult for these guns to have a line of sight to the enemy. Perhaps Greene's men had done a thorough job of cutting down the trees in front of their entrenchments and this allowed the gunners to see. The far left batteries of the Confederate position would have been the closest to Culp's Hill and logically would have responded to the fire. This would have been Captain C. I. Raine's Lee (Virginia) Battery and Captain William F. Dement's 1st Maryland Battery. These gunners suffered severely, along with the rest of Latimer's battalion. Corporal Samuel Thompson, with the 1st Maryland, was a native of Baltimore and was considered by his comrades as a very carefree and happy fellow. Sam Thompson, whose job was to carry ammunition from the caisson to the gunners, had a bad habit of leaving the lid on the ammunition chest open. He had been warned repeatedly that this was not a very safe activity, but he would simply reply, "Oh nothing's going to hurt Sam! Sam's going to Baltimore!" Within seconds of speaking these words during the cannonade, a shell exploded near the open lid of the caisson. Sparks flew in all directions, some landing in the open ammunition chest, causing a thunderous explosion! As the smoked cleared, a scene of destruction appeared. The remnants of the caisson and ammunition chest covered the ground. Wheels were splinters, their axles twisted and mangled into oblivion. The horses, innocent creatures of the carnage, bucked, tangled in their harnesses, wounded from the blast. No human casualties were reported, but then, a member of the battery noticed "a form lying prone upon the ground, clothes scorched,

**One of Major Latimer's smoothbore Napoleons on Benner's Hill.**

smoking and burning, head divested of cap and exposing a bald surface where use to be a full suit of hair, whiskers singed off to the skin, eyebrows and eyelids denuded of their fringes, and the eyes set with a popped gaze, and facial expressions changed to a perfect disguise. Was he breathing? No! The body was warm and flaccid, but the spirit had flown from care and scenes of strife to seek his 'Baltimore.' It was the body of Sam Thompson, the jovial soul."

Back at the position of the Chesapeake Artillery, Private Jacob F. Cook, the number two gunner, "while inserting a charge in the piece the wheel on the odd number side was hard hit. Sergeant Brown, Smith Warrington, Phil Oldner and Henry Wilson were each severely wounded by this shot. The Sergeant stepped down to Rock Creek, close to our position, bound up his wound, and returned to jack up his gun, put on a spare wheel, and resumed firing." Still, while the men of this battery and the others in Latimer's battalion tried valiantly to fight on, the cannonade was decidedly in the Union's favor. The Confederate guns on

Seminary Ridge, although engaged, apparently did not help much, at least not for Latimer. Fairfax Downey expressed this in his book, *The Guns at Gettysburg*, writing:

> The "Boy Major's" cannon had been given neither support nor relief by other units of Ewell's artillery. Inexplicably Carter's and Nelson's battalions had not been brought into action but stood idle in their positions north of Gettysburg. It was one of those failures by the Confederates to exert the full strength of the gunners' arm, failures which characterize the battle.

Latimer's position was becoming decidedly untenable. Realizing this, he sent word to General Johnson of his precarious position. Johnson filed the following in his Official Report:

> Major Latimer having reported to me that the exhausted condition of his horses and men, together with the terrible fire of the enemy's artillery, rendered his position untenable, he ordered to cease firing and withdraw all of his pieces excepting four, which were left in position to cover the advance of my infantry.

Johnson may have wanted four pieces to cover his infantry advance, but most other Confederate accounts stated that the four guns were to stop an advance of the enemy's infantry. Colonel J. Thompson Brown, commander of the Artillery Reserve of the Second Corps, reported, "Major Latimer was forced to withdraw three of his batteries, leaving one to repel any advance of their infantry." Lieutenant Colonel Andrews, having recovered from his wound, wrote the Official Report of the battalion, stating that the guns were withdrawn, "leaving four guns on the hill to repel any advance of the enemy's infantry."

**Some of Latimer's rifled guns on Benner's Hill.**

Robert Stiles, who witnessed Latimer's fight, wrote:

> Never, before or after, did I see fifteen or twenty guns in such a condition of wreck and destruction as this battalion was. It had been hurled backward, as it were, by the very weight and impact of metal from the position it had occupied on the crest of the little ridge, into a saucer-shaped depression behind it; and such a scene as it presented—guns dismounted and disabled, carriages splintered and crushed, ammunition chest exploded, limbers upset, wounded horses plunging and kicking, dashing out the brains of men tangled in the harness; while cannoneers with pistols were crawling around through the wreck shooting the struggling horses to save the lives of wounded men.

Wainwright, who thought he was disadvantaged, said, "Still we were able to shut them up, and actually drive them from the field in about two hours." The results of the contest meant that if the Confederates wanted to take

Culp's Hill, their infantry would have to do it without support. The uneven artillery fight was almost over, but for one more incident.

As Latimer was supervising the withdrawal of his guns from the hill, he rode back to its crest to direct the fire of the four that remained. A shell suddenly exploded near him, throwing Latimer and his horse to the ground. The animal was dead, crushing the young officer beneath its carcass. The "Boy Major" tried to pull himself free, but could not. Those around him had to lift the horse and drag the Major out. He was wounded in the arm and it was mortal. Like the hopes of the Confederacy, Latimer would die on Lee's retreat from Gettysburg.

# 5

# THE ADVANCE

Lee actually wrote two Official Reports of the battle, one on July 31, 1863, and the other in January 1864. The report of July 1863 was just an outline of events, sent to Confederate President Jefferson Davis. In it, concerning Ewell's assault, he simply stated "General Ewell attacked directly the high ground on the enemy's right, which had already been partially fortified." The January Report of 1864 was more detailed, as it was his official version of the battle of Gettysburg. This report stated "General Ewell was instructed to make a simultaneous demonstration upon the enemy's right, to be converted into a real attack should opportunity offer." Ewell's mission then seemed straightforward, to make "a simultaneous demonstration" with Longstreet's main attack.

Ewell had followed orders. Latimer's guns opened at about 4:00 P.M. (Ewell reported 5:00 P.M.) and within two hours the Federal guns had wrecked the Confederate artillery. Ewell was not done, however, as Johnson's division, minus the Stonewall Brigade, began to advance to attack Culp's Hill. Ewell, strangely, recorded:

> Immediately after the artillery firing ceased, which was just before sundown, General Johnson ordered forward his division to attack the wooded hill in his front, and about dusk the attack was made.

This report by Ewell is strange only in the sense that he said Johnson ordered his division forward and not himself. Ewell makes the assumption that we know how all that works. Johnson clarified this in his report by saying "In obedience to an order from the lieutenant-general commanding, I then advanced my infantry to the assault of the enemy's strong position." As the sun was going down, Rebel soldiers, some of whom had waited twenty-four hours to go into battle, finally formed-up and started to advance.

They were where they had halted the night before, north of the Hanover Road, with Culp's Hill a mile or so in their front. Jones's brigade, as we know, had moved to the left rear of the artillery for their support. Four companies of the 25th Virginia, of that brigade, and the 1st North Carolina had been skirmishing well forward of the division's main line, for most of the day. Later in the afternoon the remainder of the 25th Virginia joined their comrades on the skirmish line.

The skirmishing was deadly. Troops worked in groups of four, well forward of their respective battle lines. The work demanded the men to be independent, to use their own initiative. The idea was, of course, to harass the enemy, but also to feel the opposition out, determining the size of the force confronting the main line.

General Greene sent a skirmish line out very early, if not immediately, upon arriving at Culp's Hill in the morning. Lieutenant Colonel John C. O. Redington of the 60th New York commanded this mixed group of men from all the regiments in the brigade, which numbered 7 officers and 170 men. Redington reported that his men "covered the entire front of the Second Division. We advanced beyond the brook, and held our line until the advance of the line of battle of the enemy, about 7 P.M." Being a good soldier and knowing his work, Redington found the easiest places to ford Rock Creek and covered them. He said he also sent out scouts forward of the skirmish line to obtain information.

No doubt that these men made contact with the 25th Virginia and 1st North Carolina.

We can put the time then, since the artillery fight was over, at about 6:00 P.M. There was relative silence on this part of the field, except for the popping of the skirmishers and a single cannon firing here or there. Other parts of the field where Longstreet was attacking was anything but silent, as the battle progressed at all those familiar places to students of the battle: Little Round Top, the Devil's Den, the Wheatfield, and the Peach Orchard. In fact, the battle was raging in all its fury there. Meade was in desperate need of reinforcements to stop the onslaught of "Old Pete" Longstreet. Meade then committed his absolutely, undeniably, biggest mistake of the battle. He ordered the Twelfth Corps off Culp's Hill and directed them to move to the Union left. Some historians have called it "suicide"—and it was!

This shifting of the corps from their entrenched position to the opposite flank unleashed a bizarre chain of events. Much of it is open for conjecture, which is why Edwin B. Coddington, in the work of his life, wrote that Gettysburg was "a fatal attraction." The incident is clouded by emotions from the participants, but simple facts do shine through the haze.

The convoluted command structure of the Twelfth Corps, caused by the defunct "Pipe Creek Circular," has already been discussed. In summary, General Slocum somehow was under the delusion that he commanded not only his Twelfth Corps, but also the Fifth, in a fictitious right wing. Adding more cooks to the kitchen, Brigadier General Henry H. Lockwood's brigade showed up on the battlefield, on July 2, and was assigned to the Twelfth Corps. Lockwood's troops came from the defenses of Baltimore and south Maryland and were not highly regarded, having very little field experience. Because he outranked many of the generals in the Twelfth Corps, it added to the unresolved question of, who commanded whom?

Then Meade gave his order for the corps to march to the left, but it is not clear how much of the Twelfth Corps he asked for initially. He simply stated in his Official Report, "During the heavy assault upon our extreme left, portions of the Twelfth Corps were sent as re-enforcements." Slocum said that Meade ordered the entire corps off the hill, but that he (Slocum) insisted that a division should remain on the right. Williams stated that Slocum ordered him to move a division. Williams moved the First Division from Culp's Hill, which now included Lockwood's brigade, and reported to Slocum's headquarters on Power's Hill. Williams explained to Slocum that he "had great fear the rebels would seize upon our line on the right the moment we left it." Williams said that he retained Geary's Second Division at Culp's Hill, feeling that the corps could not spare more troops and safely defend the hill. Williams remarked that Slocum's response was that the "call for rein-forcements was urgent for all the troops he could spare, but he approved" of Williams suggestion that at a minimum, Geary's division was needed to guard the hill.

The sequence of the story now has Williams marching off with the First Division, confident that Culp's Hill was pro-tected. Geary's Second Division, however, proceeded onward, under orders to follow Williams and the First Division. To add more confusion to the saga, Geary's divi-sion marched completely out of the battle! They followed the First Division at least a half-hour later and got lost in the darkness. Instead of marching due west, Geary's two brigades, minus Greene, took a left turn on the Baltimore Pike and headed southeast toward Littlestown.

The question, however, remains: Who ordered Geary to move? The truth may never be known, and we can only answer with assumptions based on available evidence. Lieutenant Colonel Hiram G. Rogers, adjutant general of Slocum's staff, became a major player in the drama at this moment. Slocum related that he immediately obeyed Meade's orders to move the entire Twelfth Corps to the left, and that the corps was already in motion. Slocum, in the same moment, sent Colonel Rogers with instructions to Meade "that the enemy was in my front, and that I deemed it very hazardous to leave our entrenchments entirely undefended, and that I hoped he would permit me to retain at least a division."

Rogers quickly returned to his corps commander with a response from Meade, who stated that the emergency was on the left, but if Slocum thought it necessary, he could leave a brigade on the hill. The necessary unit to cover the Union army's right flank was General George Sears Greene's New York Brigade.

Who's to blame? Williams blamed Slocum for not retaining Geary's division on the hill. Slocum blamed Meade for this episode and all subsequent disputes that were to follow involving the Twelfth Corps at Gettysburg. For the saga did not end here. The officers of the Twelfth Corps leveled heated accusations of purposeful neglect and wrongdoing on the commanding general. Meade would not admit to any mistakes, but did amend his Official Report, attempting to rectify matters. All that, however, happened later.

Common sense, combined with hindsight, should lead to the conclusion that Meade was absolutely wrong to weaken his right flank. The bizarre command structure in the Twelfth Corps compounded the problem. A commanding officer is charged with the responsibility for the conduct and disposition of the troops under his command. In Meade's case, he happened to be the general commanding the army and therefore, as the boss, he is to be held accountable.

Although the actual time of the Twelfth Corps departure from the hill is not clear, it presented a signal to Confederates that a possible opening on the Union right existed. Those Confederate skirmishers, forward of their main line, could feel the fire slacking in their front and as was their duty, must have reported it. General Meade wrote in his amended Official Report of February 1864: "The enemy, perceiving the withdrawal of our troops, advanced and attacked General Greene."

Returning to the esteemed biographer of the Army of Northern Virginia, Douglas Southall Freeman, we read: "What he (Ewell) saw in the bombardment to think it held promise of a successful infantry attack, neither he nor anyone else ever explained."

The "promise of a successful infantry attack," however, is explained. Meade has made it clear, "The enemy, perceiving the withdrawal of our troops, advanced and attacked." Remembering General Lee's explicit orders, Ewell "was instructed to make a simultaneous demonstration upon the enemy's right, to be converted into a real attack should opportunity offer." Ewell was following Lee's directive within the confines of his orders. He made a "demonstration" against the enemy's right, "simultaneous" with Longstreet's main assault. The demonstration may not have been a good one; in fact, it could be called a disaster. Latimer's guns were wrecked, but Ewell had made a "demonstration." Harry Pfanz writes in *Gettysburg: Culp's Hill & Cemetery Hill*, "It was time for the second phase of his (Johnson's) demonstration—the infantry attack." Nowhere in the Official Reports or anywhere else is it stated that Ewell's demonstration had two phases, that is, an artillery bombardment and then an infantry attack. The removal of the Twelfth Corps in his front now provided an "opportunity," and Ewell was converting it "into a real attack." Even Freeman pointed out, "Ewell decided to turn the demonstration into an assault." After the withdrawal of the Union skirmishers, Charles Fennell wrote, "The opportunity to convert the demonstration on the Union right into a real attack had just presented itself, and the Confederates under the command of General Johnson seized the opportunity to attack."

Colonel Lewis Stegman of the Twelfth Corps wrote that when the men of his corps departed:

the strong force of skirmishers which had covered their fronts were also withdrawn, the men rejoining their respective regiments, and proceeding with the main bodies to the relief of the left wing. It should be recalled that this skirmish line had been observing the enemy all day long, and at the same time had been observed by the enemy. When it was suddenly called back, it must have attracted the attention of the enemy at once, and efforts to discover the cause have been made. This would reveal that the main force had been withdrawn, and that only a part of the troops originally stationed on the line were in occupation of this hill. Alert officers on the Confederate skirmish line could and probably did convey this important information to the commanders on Benner's Hill.

For too long students of the battle have confused Ewell's attack as a "demonstration." To characterize the Confederates' attempt to seize Culp's Hill on July 2 as a "demonstration," and not an "attack," is a misunderstanding of the facts.

Ewell's tactics for the attack were much like Longstreet's on the Union left, in the sense that it was *en echelon*, or in step-like fashion. Once Johnson's division was engaged, Early's division was to strike East Cemetery Hill. At the lower level, Johnson's brigades would attack Culp's Hill *en echelon*. Jones's brigade would lead the assault, ascending the eastern slope of the hill, where the grade was steepest, followed by the brigades of Williams (Nicholls) and "Maryland" Steuart. Johnson also reported that Walker's Stonewall Brigade was "directed to follow, but reporting to me that the enemy were advancing upon him from their right, he was ordered to repulse them and follow on as soon as possible."

Lacking the 1,450 men of the Stonewall Brigade, Johnson would send approximately 4,000 men in his advance. Their march would progress in a straight line, moving in a south-westerly direction, from the southern tip of Benner's Hill to the eastern slope of Culp's Hill. It was critical that each brigade remain in contact with others, so that the full weight of the attack could be delivered. This would require some sophisticated maneuvering, owing to the rough nature of the terrain, not to mention Yankee skirmishers. Colonel Lewis Stegman of the Twelfth Corps stated that the Confederates advanced "three lines deep." He also noted that Johnson was cognizant that the Union force on Culp's Hill was now depleted. How much depleted, however, remained an uncertainty. Stegman wrote:

> His (Johnson's) whole force in the attacks was con-centrated directly upon this point. He made no attempt to spread his lines to cover the corps posi-tion.

Three lines deep and concentrated to attack a distinct point, the Confederates would advance in a compact for-mation, marching a distance of less than a mile. They would be facing skirmishers over rough ground, while crossing Rock Creek and then ascending a steep hill.

The Confederates were aware that the Yankees had been strengthening their defenses throughout the day, as a Louisiana soldier attested, "we heard the chopping of trees on the hill; it is evident the enemy were building a line of entrenchments." Still, they could not have known how for-midable these defenses were, until they came close to them. The sun that had baked them throughout the day was falling. As they looked up at the heights to be stormed, some must have had a sinking, empty feeling, wondering how it would all go. They were veterans, good men, and they would do their duty, but the intensity amongst the men in the lines must have been thick as a morning fog.

General Jones's men stepped off first, marching down the rather steep slope of Benner's Hill. Jones wrote, "As the brigade advanced, a few shells were thrown from the batteries on the right, though but little damage resulted from them." It would not take long for those guns to lose sight of the Confederates as they passed into the woods surrounding Rock Creek. Colonel Wainwright related an incident that probably occurred when the two forces were fully engaged, but nonetheless, explained the lack of artillery support for Union arms:

> General Wadsworth sent over to know if I could not fire into the woods so as to strike the enemy. I sent back word that I could not without endangering our own men. Wadsworth then came over himself, and pointed out the spot where he said the rebs were and where he wanted to fire. I still insisted that it was within our lines, but he said that he had just come from there, and knew exactly where our lines were. I had been over there in the morning, and thought differently. But not wishing to be ugly, I had one of "L" Company's guns pointed there, and then insisted on Wadsworth's aiming himself at the point he wanted to hit. So soon as he had seen one shot fired, he galloped off, quite happy. I had that gun fire slowly, watching it myself, for I could not believe I had made so great a mistake in spotting our position on the hill. We had not fired half a dozen shots when a major of the Twelfth Corps came over and said that we were dropping every shot directly into their line, and had already disabled half a dozen men. It was just as I supposed, the rebs were around the corner, where I could not get at them.

Greene's men, like the Confederate infantry, would be without artillery support in their fight on Culp's Hill.

Jones and Williams's Louisiana brigade reached Rock Creek with relative ease. Steuart, however, had problems

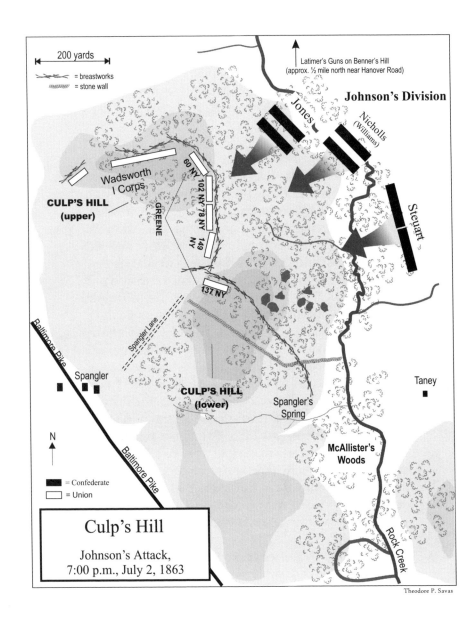

200 yards

= breastworks
= stone wall

Latimer's Guns on Benner's Hill
(approx. ½ mile north near Hanover Road)

**Johnson's Division**

Jones

Nicholls
(Williams)

Steuart

Wadsworth
I Corps

**CULP'S HILL
(upper)**

GREENE

60 NY

102 NY

78 NY

149 NY

137 NY

Spangler Lane

Spangler

N

Baltimore Pike

Baltimore Pike

**CULP'S HILL
(lower)**

Spangler's
Spring

Taney

**McAllister's
Woods**

Rock Creek

= Confederate
= Union

# Culp's Hill

Johnson's Attack,
7:00 p.m., July 2, 1863

Theodore P. Savas

aligning his brigade to strike the target and keeping contact with the left of Williams. He was "obliged to swing around by a right half-wheel, and the brigade thus formed front toward the west by south." This difficult maneuver, under fire from Greene's skirmishers, while crossing the bend in Rock Creek, caused his brigade to split into two wings. Steuart related:

> The right wing of the brigade crossed the creek considerably in advance of the center and left wing, owing to the fact that the order to move by a right half-wheel was not immediately understood on the left, and also to the greater number of natural obstacles to be overcome by that part of the brigade.

The 3rd North Carolina and the 1st Maryland Battalion "were now entirely separated from the rest of the brigade." Steuart's command was having problems even before they reached Greene's main line.

Greene's main line of battle existed, however, by what Hannibal called "the might of Fortune and chances of war." Meade's biggest mistake had been committed, the fate of the battle hung in the balance, and luck had shifted its weight to the Confederates. Meade's blunder was Lee's best chance. The attack on Culp's Hill, on the night of July 2, constituted Lee's greatest opportunity for victory in the battle of Gettysburg. The gods of war, however, had placed the oldest, toughest, most determined officer, along with his men, between "the birth of a new nation" and Southern Independence.

The somewhat accidental retention of Greene's New York Brigade on the threatened flank gave cause for the emergence of another forgotten hero to the drama. As the Confederates began their advance, the Twelfth Corps was exiting the stage, yet the fire of the skirmishers was increasing. The Rebels were attacking and orders to clarify Greene's defense were needed. Entering the play in this critical scene, for his second cameo appearance was Lieutenant Colonel Hiram C. Rogers. The story is given to us by one of Greene's staff:

> I think it must have been about 6 P.M. when we received orders to move out of our works and reinforce the line on the left. My brigade being on the left of the corps, was the last to leave. They were actually in march, and orders had been sent to draw in our skirmishers, when a message was received from the officer in command of the skirmishers that the enemy in heavy force had quitted the woods in which they had lain all day, and were moving on our front apparently 5 or 6,000 strong.
>
> General Greene halted his brigade, reinforced the skirmish line, ordered the officer in command to make a short fight, at the same time reporting his action to Gen. Geary who had left at the head of his division. Gen. Geary, on receiving the report declined to confirm Gen. Greene's advice and ordered the brigade to follow the march of the 2d and 1st Brigades at once. Very fortunately Lieut. Col. (Hiram C.) Rodgers, A.A.G. to Gen. Slocum, passing at that time met an officer charged with Gen. Geary's orders and directing him to order Gen. Greene to remain where he was promised to Gen. Geary with the 1st and 2d Brigades directly back to the works he had quitted. By the time the officer charged with this order had reached Gen. Greene, the skirmishers were falling slowly back, closely pushed by the enemy and withdrawal would have been almost impossible.

In the large cast of characters in the great battle, only a few have maintained leading roles. Lieutenant Colonel Rodgers and his efforts have long since been forgotten, but his role was critical to Greene's defense.

Colonel Stegman recorded Greene's original alignment of his regiments:

> On the hill, joining Wadsworth's division, was the Seventy-eighth, then the Sixtieth, part of its front down the hill; the One hundred and second, at the foot of the hill, forming the center; the One hundred and forty-ninth next, while the right of the brigade was occupied by the One hundred and thirty-seventh.

Lieutenant Colonel Redington was, as stated, working the brigade skirmish line. The 137th New York, commanded by Colonel David Ireland, was now the end of the line on the Union army's right. Edward Bearss, living legend Civil War Guide and historian, has referred to the 20th Maine and 137th New York as "the bookend regiments."

Jones recalled that his men "advanced in good order," crossed Rock Creek and went up the hill "occupied by the enemy." This seems too easy as others had much more to say. Captain Jesse M. Richardson, commanding the 42nd Virginia, related that his men marched "in splendid line" as they advanced. He said a "temporary halt was made at the creek at the foot of the mountain, where the regiment suffered some from the enemy's shells, which had been harmless until the creek was reached." The Confederates, after the battle, loved to refer to Culp's Hill as a "mountain."

It seems Jones's men stopped at Rock Creek, reformed, and prepared to cross the obstacle. Colonel Redington "immediately withdrew" his skirmishers to the other side of the creek and threw forward his reserves, putting every man he had into the fight. Ever so slowly they fell back, Redington proudly stating the men behaved "in a truly splendid manner." Now he opened fire with all the might he could muster and the enemy appeared to "lie down in the grass." He intended to form his line about a hundred yards from the bank of the creek, where he knew the

Confederates would try to cross. From this point, he would attempt to "sweep them as they crossed." Redington sent a runner to find the 28th Pennsylvania and tell that regiment's commander to move up and assist. They would not come, however, having left the hill in the corps march to the left.

Redington, realizing his thin skirmisher line was about to be overwhelmed, gave the bugle call for help and Greene responded immediately by sending out the 78th New York to his assistance.

Lieutenant Colonel Herbert von Hammerstein, commander of the 78th, filed his regiment to the right and marched in the rear of the 60th New York. The 78th then passed through the lines of the 102nd and advanced to the vacated position of the 28th Pennsylvania.

This unusual maneuvering of the 78th New York is enlightening. Rather than advancing directly forward from the crest of the hill, where the slope was extremely steep, the 78th, not yet under fire, chose to descend the hill where the incline was not so acute. The position they vacated was exactly the point of attack for Jones's Virginians. It seems almost folly, with the benefit of hindsight, that troops would attempt to assault such a steep incline against an entrenched enemy. An apparently impossible task faced the Virginians.

The reinforcement of Redington's 177 men by Hammerstein's 200 did little to stop the Rebel horde, as the Confederates made a rush at them. Some Confederates, however, did think enough of the blue skirmishers to call it a "front line." Captain T. R. Buckner of the 44th Virginia simply stated, "Crossing a creek at the foot of the mountain, we charged up the hill, driving the enemy before us." Colonel John C. Higginbotham, commanding the 25th Virginia, said the Yankee skirmishers "made but feeble resistance, until thrown back upon their line of support"; the Virginians dislodged them in but one charge. This again, however, is an inadequate description of the facts.

Redington recorded that the fighting was so close he captured twelve prisoners!

The skirmish line, however, bought General Greene time to receive the amended orders from Colonel Rogers and time to begin stretching his line to cover as much of the empty trenches as possible. The 137th New York began shifting to their right, filling in the works left vacant by General Kane's missing brigade. The other regiments in Greene's brigade followed suit, from right to left. Before the men had time to complete the shift, however, the Confederates of Jones's brigade struck the 60th New York, now Greene's left regiment.

As a result of this shift, the men of Greene's brigade were at least a foot apart from each other. This was not typical Civil War tactics, as soldiers generally fired volleys while standing shoulder to shoulder. This gave them what was called "massed firepower." Greene, however, needed to give up firepower to gain ground, for it was necessary to cover a wide front. He was an excellent combat engineer, though, and he put his training to good effect. The preparations of the morning, combined with the configuration of the trench line he was to defend, gave him a great advantage for the defense.

# 6

## THE EVENING BATTLE

### Shadows, Sounds, and Flashes of Light

Darkness began to fall on the arena of the combatants; General Greene listed the time as "a few minutes before 7 P.M." As the Union skirmishers were being driven back toward the main line, the unpleasant possibility of being shot by their comrades became very real. They yelled out to them to hold their fire. Captain George K. Collins recalled the scene:

> A little after five o'clock in the afternoon a detachment of skirmishers was sent down the hill in front of the brigade line and had receded from view only a short time when they came running back followed by a Confederate line of battle, yelping and howling in its peculiar manner. Some of the skirmishers were killed in sight of the brigade, and occasionally a stray bullet came whizzing by the heads of the men in the rifle pits, who were so eager and clamorous that it was all the officers could do to prevent them from opening fire before the men in the skirmish line could come in. The skirmishers seeing their light was dimmed by the dense foliage, the woods wore a sombre hue, and all was still as death.

For the boys in blue, "moments passed which were years of agony," as they waited for the chugging Confederates to come into point-blank range. An image like that of Minutemen at Lexington Green comes to mind, with an officer shouting "Don't fire until you see the whites of their eyes," as the New Yorkers kept sweaty fingers on cold metal triggers.

Then, a crack, a pop, as firing slowly broke out, the Virginians were now seventy-five yards from Greene's main line. The Rebs were shooting as they gained altitude, climbing the steep slope, but their missiles mostly knocked into the wood and stones of the breastworks. Colonel Horton of Greene's staff recalled:

> In the gathering gloom of the evening, the line held by Greene's brigade could scarcely be distinguished until they were within pistol range. The colors were dropped behind the works and men closely concealed.

Indeed, Horton must have been correct, as it appeared to Captain T. R. Buckner of the 44th Virginia that his men would need "scaling ladders" to surmount the Yankee fortifications.

The Confederates gained ground, just seventy yards away and firing. . . then sixty yards. . . closer to fifty-five yards. . . and then it came. A murderous volley was poured into their ranks as the woodsmen of the St. Lawrence ripped them a good one. Staggered and stunned, the Southerners continued advancing. A soldier of the 60th wrote that the men

> restrained their anxious guns with the enemy muskets spewing fire at them not fifteen yards in front. And then through the darkness came their return fire. The light from the muzzle blasts of hundreds of

Greene's muskets lit the woods like day, revealing Johnson's Confederates massed below.

As the dark consumed the hill, it now would become a battle of shadows, sounds, and flashes of light. Volley after volley now rang through the trees like thunder rolling over mountains and valleys, all down the line. Colonel Stegman reported, "For hours the crash of musketry was unceasing; three hours of conflict with rifle balls at close quarters." Men fired at what they heard, not being able to see. A shadow, caused from a flash, or the silhouette of a figure from the bright moon, would bring a shot and a ping or a thud, depending on if the lead missile hit a rock, a tree, or flesh.

Early in this attack, Colonel Higginbotham of the 25th Virginia was wounded, but stayed with his men till the firing ceased. General Jones was shot through the thigh, the "excessive hemorrhage from which rendered it necessary" for him to be "borne from the field." Eventually, Lieutenant Colonel Dungan would take command of the brigade. The 60th New York was pounding the Virginians. Colonel Goddard, commander of the 60th, related the nature of the work:

> After the opening of the infantry fire, an order was received from General Greene that I must hold the works under all circumstances. I sent frequently for ammunition, which was promptly furnished, the right being out of ammunition but one time, when, by my order bayonets were fixed, and thus remained until their boxes were replenished.

It became apparent that the Rebs could not stay so close for too long. They would fall back, reform, and try again. Benjamin Jones of the 44th Virginia penned his experience of the fight:

When the order came we crawled over the creek and rugged rocks the best we could and charged the first line and took it, but the enemy had another ditch further up the hill filled with men firing down on our heads. We could not hold what we had gained, hence were driven back for a few hundred yards from whence we could reform and charge again with like results, three times. In this charge some of my personal friends fell.

A soldier in the 60th New York vividly recalled the action in a letter to his father:

We expected to be overpowered in a short time. By this time the skirmishers had got in all who were not killed or wounded, and the enemy were close by, coming toward us slowly, firing all the time.

Not a shot was fired at them until they got within about 15 rods. Then the order was given (Fire!) and we did fire, and kept firing. If ever men loaded and fired more rapidly than the 60th did on that occasion, I never saw them do it. The rebels yelled like wild indians and charged upon us on a double quick. They acted bravely, they came as close as they could, but very few got within 2 rods of us, those that did never went away again. We gave them a welcome with leaden bullets that sent many a brave rebel, for they are brave, to his last account. Well they retreated in a hurry. . . Soon we heard the rebels coming again. Our men sprang to their places. This time they came with a rush—they had been reinforced, and thought to drive us out certain. Again death met them in the face. They charged again, and again retreated.

Captain Jesse H. Jones of the 60th New York was thankful to his creator, for he was sure that a miracle had been performed which kept him alive. While marching toward Chancellorsville, Jones came upon a pair of breastplates, essentially a bulletproof vest. He wore them in the battle at Culp's Hill and wrote how they fit him:

> The shoulder supports held them up; my blouse was buttoned up over them, and the swordbelt buckled around held them firmly to the body. They lapped by about an inch, and probably were intended to do so.

While in the heat of the fight, a Confederate fired at him about fifteen yards away. The bullet struck the outer breastplate, denting it about half an inch and then made a "hollow a quarter of an inch deep or so." He was sure he would have been killed without them.

After about two hours the Rebel fire slackened and Goddard

> ordered an advance of a portion of our regiment, who eagerly leaped the works and surrounded about 50 of the enemy, among whom were 2 officers, and took at the time two flags, one a brigade color and the other a regimental banner. At the receipt of these flags, a quiet enthusiasm pervaded the men and officers of the regiment.

As soon as the attack commenced, Greene sent a request for reinforcements from the First and Eleventh Corps posted on his left. In the meantime, Greene's New York Brigade would have to hold their ground, locked in a struggle of death, and outnumbered almost four to one— Greene's brigade numbered 1,350 and Johnson's division totaled about 4,000.

As the 60th New York fought off Jones's Virginians on the left of Greene's line, the *en echelon* attack of the Confederates became more developed. Colonel Williams's

**Monument to the 60th New York Infantry.**

Louisiana brigade, while the fighting was raging on his right, now attacked Greene's center, squaring off against the 78th and 102nd regiments and the left of the 149th New York.

Colonel Williams described the Cajuns' advance as being similar to Jones's. The brigade brushed aside the Union skirmish line and "reached a line about 100 yards from the enemy's works, when it again engaged him with an almost incessant fire for four hours."

A soldier in the ranks remembered it this way:

> [T]he enemy's pickets were soon driven in by our own, then with a yell our men rushed forward as best they could up the steep hillside over rocks and through the timber up to the enemy's line of works.

Captain Collins of the 149th New York described the incredible agony of waiting for the Confederates to get close:

The pale faces, staring eyeballs, and nervous hands grasping loaded muskets, told how terrible were those moments of suspense. At last the fire broke out. . . As each man fired, he involuntarily drew back and sought safety behind the works as if alarmed at the sound of his own musket and the murderous work he had done. After discharging one or two shots, the men regained their composure and began to load and fire more steadily and with greater rapidity.

The darkness, combined with the density of the smoke now rendered everything completely invisible. Yet, the Louisiana boys would try repeated charges against the breastworks, falling back, reforming, and giving it another go. At times they would reach right up to the works, as one of them wrote, "We had reached within but a few rods of their line, the position and the odds were against us, the fighting was continued until some time after dark." Some of the brigade would claim that the 1st Louisiana actually entered the Union side of the trenches, which is not improbable. One Rebel recounted the episode, "The right of our line, the First Louisiana, penetrated their entrenchments, but owning to the conformation of the hill and the angle of the Federal line, our troops became massed upon the center and our efforts to dislodge the enemy failed." Sergeant Charles Clancy, color-bearer of the 1st Louisiana, met a fate of many Confederates who advanced too close to the breastworks. These men would become "afraid to either advance or retreat," pinned down by the rifles of the New Yorkers. As Clancy realized his choices were death or capture, he pulled his regiment's flag from its staff and wrapped it around his body, hiding it beneath his clothes. As a prisoner, he somehow was able to conceal the flag, until he was exchanged in the winter. He returned to his regiment along with the missing flag.

**Some of the rough ground the Confederates had to face as they attacked Greene's line. A rock from Culp's Hill that the Greene family requested to be used as the general's headstone at his grave was taken from this area.**

Colonel Stegman spoke of the assaults along his front:

> Four times, with desperate yells, with the determination to carry these works at all hazards, had the Confederates charged; four times they went back discomfited. They had charged clear to the works, so close that they made attempts to grasp the regimental flags, and died as their hand clutched for the colors. They built breastworks of their own dead on this brigade front, so merciless was the Union fire; and the men who so use their comrades' bodies were killed behind them.

The fourth time might have been the charm, as Captain Nathan J. Rawlings of the 14th Louisiana wrote in his *Thrilling Experiences,* published in 1909, saying it was the hottest fight he had been in.

Three times we charged the breastworks and were
repulsed, but the fourth time we succeeded, after a
heroic struggle and the loss of many men. I was
shot in the left leg and bayoneted in the left breast.
I don't know how I got out of the breastworks, but
the next morning I was in the woods with a number
of other wounded men and our regimental physi-
cian, Dr. Campbell, was dressing my wounds.

He added, "The young folks of today don't know anything about hard times. This money panic and boll worm
problem are pleasant to what the soldiers had to stand."

Colonel Hammerstein, as previously mentioned, was
ordered to send his regiment, the 78th New York, forward
to assist Colonel Redington on the skirmish line. His men,
driven back by the wild rush of the Confederates, were
"ordered to fall in" by General Greene. The 78th New York,
as their monument on the battlefield depicts, "joined with
102nd NY" and "succeeded in repulsing a most furious
attack of the enemy." As the Louisiana brigade fell back a
last time, Hammerstein conceded that his men had
exhausted their last rounds of ammunition.

**Monument to the 78th and 102nd New York Infantries.**

Mixing with the echoes of the blasting rifles, a new sound was added to the furious rage of the bloody contest—calls from the desperate voices of the wounded. Cries of "mother, mother," and "water, water," could be heard by the soldiers of both sides. The Confederates, again, had the worst of it—their dead and wounded were too near the trenches of the enemy to be safe to retrieve them. A Virginia soldier wrote:

> In my company was a man by the name of Robert Slaughter who had a brother by the name of William in Co. H, who fell wounded near the enemy's breastworks. His brother Robert could hear him calling for water, as all wounded men do, but could afford him no relief. He died there and afterwards Robert received a fatal wound and died.

Many of the gray-clad soldiers would write later of not leaving any of their comrades, whether dead or wounded, upon the hill. This was not true, however, as a member of the 60th New York wrote that he

> heard their wounded groaning and begging for help. Many of our men went over and commenced bringing them in. Such of them as could walk came into our lines and gave themselves up.

Union troops would be assigned to the morbid duty of burying the dead of both sides. This was later, of course, when the battle was over and it became safe to leave the security of the rifle pits.

The Confederate assaults against Greene's line were similar—both Rebel brigades would charge the breastworks, only to be driven back. Once reformed, the Confederates would repeat the effort, rushing the Yankee line, only to meet with the same result against Greene's immovable line. Like Stegman, Greene reported the "enemy made four distinct charges between 7 and 9:30 P.M., which were effectually resisted." Colonel Williams complained that after maintaining an "incessant fire for four hours, pending which several attempts to carry the works by assault, being entirely unsupported on the right (Jones's brigade having failed to hold its line on the right), were attended with more loss than success." Witnessing the futility of his attacks against Greene's impregnable line, the frustration of Williams was clear. It seemed unlikely, despite his protestations, that the Louisiana men could have taken the "works," even with Jones's support. Williams and his men, as Captain Rawlings suggested, believed at one point that Greene's line had been breached. Although it is possible, it is unlikely. As his men advanced up Culp's Hill, they lost their cohesion—it was dark, the ground favored the defenders, and Greene's men poured devastating volleys into their ranks. Jones, having to advance over the worst terrain of the entire division, had his own problems and was in no position to support Williams. The Confederate officers' corps had asked the impossible of the men in the ranks.

## Trouble on the Right

While the Confederate right and center attacks suffered "more loss than success," the left flank was in a position to achieve substantial, if not decisive, results. The problem was they did not know it. "Maryland" Steuart's regiments were already quite confused in the darkness, having separated into two entirely different "wings." The right wing consisted of the 3rd North Carolina and 1st Maryland in the front line and the 1st North Carolina to the right rear of the 3rd North Carolina, as a reserve. The left wing consisted of the three Virginia regiments of the brigade, the 37th, 23rd, and 10th Virginia Infantries. These regiments of the left wing, like that of the 1st North Carolina, would appear later in the contest. Meanwhile, the 3rd North Carolina and 1st Maryland crossed Rock

Creek and ascended the "thickly wooded" smaller hill, trying to keep pace with the left of Williams's men. As they
moved into the saddle area north of the crest of the
smaller hill, they felt the wrath of the hill's defenders.
The 3rd North Carolina now "received a front and oblique
fire" from the 149th New York in its front and a devastating blow along their left flank from the 137th New York.
The configuration of the Union trench system had the 3rd
North Carolina trapped in a sideways "L" or half a box,
a crossfire that spelled complete extinction with pro-
longed exposure. The 1st Maryland quickly moved alongside the 3rd North Carolina to relieve them from the jaws
of the deadly trap. In turn, they received an invitation to
the infernal regions of hell, from an almost point-blank
shot of the 137th New York. The commander of the
Maryland troops, Lieutenant Colonel James R. Herbert, fell
from "this terrific fire," wounded three times. The pressure,
however, had been relieved on the left of the Tar Heels.
Officers with the 3rd North Carolina stated that once the
Maryland men engaged the enemy on their left, the fire in
front became heavier as they battled the 149th New York.
This seems unusual, as Colonel Henry Barnum, commander of the 149th New York, reported:

> The enemy made repeated and desperate charges
> upon our position, but was as often repulsed with
> great slaughter to him until our ammunition gave
> out, when we held the position with the bayonet
> and such limited firing as could be made with the
> ammunition of the killed and wounded.

Most likely, the entire 149th New York began to focus
their fire directly to their front, paying less attention to
Williams's brigade, which was weakening, on their left.

The battling was so great in front of the 149th New York
that twice during the fighting for Culp's Hill Color Sergeant
William C. Lilly had to splice back together the flagstaff,

which was broken by enemy bullets. After Gettysburg was over, the 149th counted eighty bullets in their colors. Sergeant Lilly is depicted on the bas-relief on the regiment's monument, which is titled, "Mending the flag."

As the 1st North Carolina moved to the support of their comrades another grave and unfortunate incident of friendly fire occurred. The episode is indicative of why there was very little night fighting in the Civil War. Lieutenant Randolph H. McKim, aide-de-camp to General Steuart and former member of 1st Maryland, was leading eight companies of the 1st North Carolina. This regiment had been placed in the rear of the Steuart's right wing, for support. McKim had been eager for action, asking Steuart repeatedly to let him lead his group forward into position. They advanced slowly toward the 3rd North Carolina and 1st Maryland. Seeing the flash of muskets in his front and feeling the whiz of minié balls all around him, McKim ordered the 1st North Carolina to fire. In the darkness and smoke, McKim had mistaken his friends for the enemy. His men were firing on the 3rd North Carolina and McKim's old regiment, the 1st Maryland. Major William M. Parsley, commander of the 3rd North Carolina, ran down the hill and told McKim to stop firing as they were shooting their own men.

McKim, who became a priest in the Episcopal Church soon afterward, believed that his error did not cause much damage. He later wrote

"Owing to the din of battle the command to fire had not been heard except by those nearest to me, and I believe no injury resulted from my mistake. I mention it only to assume the responsibility for the order."

However, the observation of Major Goldsborough was somewhat different. He stated that

> the First North Carolina, which was marching in reserve, believing they were being fired upon by the enemy, opened fire, by which a number of men in the two right regiments were killed and wounded.

McKim's honesty was honorable, even if his perspective was slanted.

Division commander Johnson seemed to be nearby, although the whereabouts of Ewell are unclear, as Steuart reported that Johnson ordered him to "advance our left wing as rapidly and as steadily as possible." The three Virginia regiments of the left wing had a longer distance to travel than those on the right, caused by the brigade's swinging door, "right half wheel" maneuver. In addition, these regiments advanced over rougher terrain, the left actually passing over the western base of Wolf's Hill. After Johnson's order, Steuart brought them into the action in the area of the smaller hill.

The 23rd Virginia, commanded by Lieutenant Colonel Simeon Walton, advanced steadily and climbed the east slope of the smaller hill. The Virginians were now near the empty trenches of the Twelfth Corps and had unknowingly gained the flank of the 137th New York. Greene had trouble on his right.

The fight at Culp's Hill became extremely confusing for the participants at this point. The Confederates were trampling on unfamiliar ground, in the dark, in the face of an enemy

**A view from the traverse, looking into the valley or saddle, the scene of intense action during the course of the fighting.**

whose awareness was only slightly better. The Confederates were blind to the fact that the rear of the Union army lay open. Instead of passing by the right of the 137th New York and advancing 500 yards to the Baltimore Pike, they chose to fight it out in the darkness. They should be excused for this, because good soldiers generally "march to the sound of the guns." Woe, however, for the loss of the Stonewall Brigade! The 10th Virginia, the far-left regiment of the division, was at that very moment marching through Pardee Field with nothing to stop them. The great "what ifs" of Gettysburg should include the failure of the Stonewall Brigade to advance, presumably on the left, of Johnson's division on the night of July 2. Although the question arises of how much damage they truly could have done, a brigade, or more, in Meade's rear would have offered grave consequences.

Unaware in the darkness of what lay in his front, Walton sent a scout to investigate. Sure enough, Yankees were close by, about twenty yards in his front. Walton walked around to his right for he knew assistance lurked somewhere in the area. He soon found Major W. W. Goldsborough, who at the moment was unaware that he was in command of the 1st Maryland, owing to Colonel Herbert's wounding. The Maryland men had been "ordered to lie down scarcely thirty yards from the enemy's breastworks." They were a hundred yards from the angle where Greene's trenchline met Kane's. Some of them would later describe their predicament:

> While lying down, we could distinctly see the Federals rise and fire at us from the works in front. Indeed, they fought so stubbornly, that orders passed up the line that we were firing into our own men, and we began to think that it was Longstreet coming up from the other side.

Walton asked Goldsborough if he could not join the 23rd Virginia in a charge upon the Yankees. Goldsborough

131

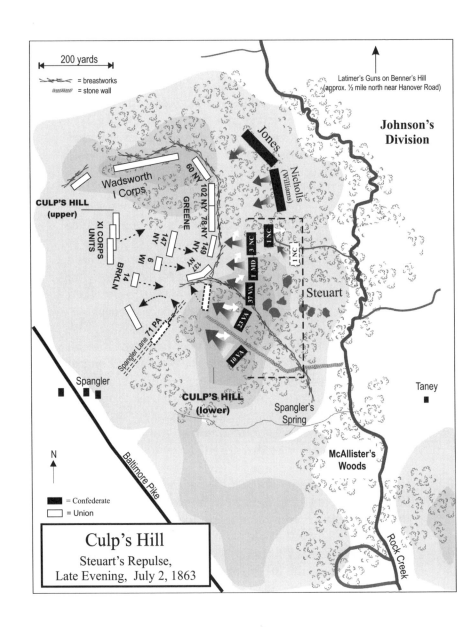

200 yards

= breastworks
= stone wall

Latimer's Guns on Benner's Hill
(approx. ½ mile north near Hanover Road)

Johnson's
Division

Jones

Nicholls
(Williams)

Wadsworth
I Corps

60 NY

102 NY

78 NY

149

CULP'S HILL
(upper)

GREENE

XI CORPS
UNITS

147
NY

9
WI

1 NC

3 NC

1 NC

137
NY

1 MD

BRKLN

14

37 VA

Steuart

Spangler Lane 71 PA

23 VA

10 VA

Spangler

CULP'S HILL
(lower)

Spangler's
Spring

Taney

N

McAllister's
Woods

= Confederate
= Union

Culp's Hill
Steuart's Repulse,
Late Evening, July 2, 1863

Baltimore Pike

Rock Creek

obliged by shifting his three left companies, the participants explaining:

> After lying in this position probably fifteen minutes, we were ordered to charge, and as we climbed over the breastworks we distinctly remember seeing dead or wounded Yankees within the works.

The Union main line had been breached. This is the only time in the entire battle that Confederate troops successfully gained—and held—a portion of the now famous "fish hook."

The 23rd Virginia now filed right, "until it reached the portion of the breastworks which was at right angles to the part first captured. Forming in line on the flank and almost in rear of the enemy, there stationed, it opened fire upon them, killing, wounding, and capturing quite a number." The 23rd Virginia had reached the crest of the lower hill, a position that dominated the area in the lower saddle.

Greene's left regiments may have been holding the Rebels in check, but the desperate position of the 137th New York threatened his entire line. The Confederates had an opportunity to roll up Greene's flank like a carpet. Fortunately, the man responsible for holding down the right possessed the imperturbable constitution of a mighty and fearless warrior. This man, of course, was Colonel David Ireland, commander of the 137th New York.

Ireland recorded the time as 8:00 P.M. when he first detected enemy movement on his right. If Ireland and Greene had synchronized their watches, which is doubtful, the brigade had been under fire for a little over an hour. Ireland gave ground sparingly, contesting every inch. He refused his right-flank company, Company A, bending them back in a manner much the same as the 20th Maine on Little Round Top. Hence, the "bookend regiments" were both forced to refuse their lines to stave off enemy attacks against their flanks.

A view from the bottom of the valley or saddle, looking up at Greene's traverse. The rock with plaque in its front is the monument to the 14th Brooklyn. This marks the spot where the Union trench formed a right angle (in the right center of the photo) and where Greene built his traverse. The rock of the 14th Brooklyn notes the location of the traverse.

A view from the traverse looking at the right angle formed by the Union trenchline. The valley between the larger and smaller hill is on the right.

Ireland recorded the events:

> The enemy advanced on our right flank. At this time I ordered Company A, the right-flank company, to form at right angles with the breastworks, and check the advance of the enemy.

Company A now faced the 23rd Virginia, and tried stubbornly to hold them back. Ireland continued the account:

> ... they did for some time, but, being sorely pressed, they fell back a short distance to a better position, and there remained until Lieutenant Cantine, of General Greene's staff, brought up a regiment of the First Corps. I placed them in the position occupied by Company A, but they remained there but a short time.

## Reinforcements

The regiment of the First Corps to which Ireland was referring was the 71st Pennsylvania, nicknamed "the California Regiment," and was, in fact, part of the Second Corps. General Greene, who seemed ubiquitous, had called for reinforcements as soon as the attack began. Although, he asked assistance from the First and Eleventh Corps, those units closest to him, the Second Corps was one of the first to respond. General Winfield S. Hancock, nicknamed "the Superb," had heard the firing on the right, his trained ear telling him that the Twelfth Corps needed help. He sent two regiments; the 71st and 106th Pennsylvania. The 106th headed for Cemetery Hill, but the 71st came like the cavalry in the nick of time, when Ireland was being pressed.

The 71st's arrival was not, however, so gallant, for it appears that they came to the right place, at the right time, only because they were lost. Colonel Richard Penn Smith, the regiment's commander, explained:

> About dark of this day, by an order through
> Captain Duffy, I was ordered to the support of a
> portion of the Eleventh Corps. Having arrived on
> the ground, I could find no general to report to who
> had command of any one portion of the troops. An
> adjutant-general directed me to proceed to the
> front, assuring me that all was safe on either flank.
> Arriving at the front, I became engaged with the
> enemy on the front. At the same time he attacked
> me on my right and rear.

Colonel Smith somehow, in the dark, marched off to the
right. There, he bumped into Captain Craig W. Wadsworth,
who guided him to Greene's rear. Wadsworth then handed
over the 71st Pennsylvania to Colonel Horton, Greene's
adjutant. The situation called for immediate reinforcements, and it did not matter who they were. Horton
escorted the 71st Pennsylvania to the desperate situation
unfolding along the right of the 137th New York.
Colonel Smith reported:

> I immediately ordered my command to retire to the
> road in my rear, when I returned to camp against
> orders. During the engagement, I lost 3 commis-
> sioned offers and 11 enlisted men.

Smith retreated from the position, without orders!
Horton was shocked and wrote of the incident:

> The regiment however was very slow in coming up,
> and again rode back to hurry them it up. They
> finally advanced and went into the trenches giving
> three loud cheers as they reached them. These
> cheers were answered by a few scattering shots
> from the front and from the right front, by which I
> do not think any injury was inflicted. A few shots
> were also fired, I think by the Regt., which immedi-

ately to my astonishment rose up and retreated in line, apparently without panic or disorder. Riding up to the Colonel I found that he had ordered the retreat, saying that he would not have his men murdered, and that he lost several men by the fire &c., which I believe to be untrue. I urged him forward but he informed me that he received orders to return to his corps and he thereupon marched to the rear to the sound of the enemy's guns.

Sergeant William J. Burns of Company G, 71st Pennsylvania, wrote:

it was a blunder on the part of our officers and came near costing us dear. It was the heaviest and wickedest musketry firing for about half an hour that ever I lay under.

It should be noted that the 71st Pennsylvania would see action at the climax of Pickett's Charge at the famous "Angle." Their performance there is also questionable, as it was on this night. Sergeant Burns's statement that the firing near the 137th New York "was the heaviest and wickedest . . . ever I lay under" is testament to how fierce the struggle at Culp's Hill really was.

At about the same moment as the 71st Pennsylvania was heading to the 137th right, the other reinforcements that General Greene had requested were arriving. The First Corps sent the 6th Wisconsin of the famous Iron Brigade, the 14th Brooklyn, nicknamed "the Red Legged Devils," and the 147th New York. The Eleventh Corps sent four regiments, the 45th and 157th New York, the 61st Ohio, and the 82nd Illinois. All of these units had seen heavy action the previous day, still Greene estimated that their strengths added about 755 men to his ranks.

The 1st Maryland and 37th and 10th Virginia had now joined the 23rd Virginia, and they blasted Ireland from the front and right flank, possibly even hitting his rear. These Confederates formed a battle line from the just-captured breastworks on the crest of the lower hill to the stone wall that runs along the border of Pardee field. Ireland was now pressed to the limit, without any help. Steuart described the action from this position:

> It was enabled to open a cross-fire upon the enemy, doing considerable execution. More, however, might have been done had not the impression at this time prevailed that we were firing upon our friends, and the fire been discontinued at intervals.

Again, the Rebels were thwarted from achieving decisive results. Their fire was sporadic due to the confusion caused by the darkness. The 10th Virginia, whose right was being guided by the stone wall, was now ordered to perform a sortie to determine whether friend or foe was in front. They changed front and faced the wall and moved by the left flank along it. They had now gained the 137th New York rear and opened fire. It was all that Ireland and his men

**The stone wall used by the 10th Virginia to guide them into the valley. Pardee Field is on the left.**

could stand. There was, however, fortunately for the dogged and determined boys of the Excelsior State, a saving grace. They retired to the once seemingly superfluous traverse that General Greene had ordered them to build. Greene's training as an engineer now paid dividends for the lives of his men. Ireland was able to hold "the enemy in check" from this right-angled extension of the line of breastworks.

The 137th New York's fighting withdrawal to the traverse caused the exposure of the 149th New York's right flank. Colonel Barnum, commander of the 149th, attempted to shift the facing of his three right companies to counter this threat. The movement required the regiment to fall back slightly and Barnum thought his line officers understood the order. In the execution of the movement, however, part of the regiment retreated. This violated the theory of the "military crest," and placed the men on the highest ground, to the rear of the pits. Barnum explained,

> This movement was executed under a most galling fire and when wholly exposed, as the ground a short distance to the rear of the works was elevated so as to give full range to the enemy's musketry.

The situation was quickly rectified as an order was given for the men to move forward and reoccupy the trenches. It seems likely, however, that during this movement a few Confederates took advantage of the 149th's confusion and entered the breastworks. The 6th Wisconsin, led by Lieutenant Colonel Rufus Dawes, had just recently arrived on the hill and Dawes, luckily, ran into none other than General Greene, himself.

Dawes left us an account of his war experiences, titled *Service with the Sixth Wisconsin Volunteers*. It is truly one of the classic memoirs of the Civil War. Here is the excerpt describing his exploits on Culp's Hill:

> We started for General Greene. Who he was I did not know, but the musketry showed where to go. The first mounted officer I saw proved to be General G. S. Greene, of the Twelfth Army Corps. Taking from his pocket a card, he wrote in the darkness his name and command, which he handed to me. He then directed me to form my regiment, and go into the breastworks; to go as quickly as possible, and to hold the works after I got there. I did not then understand, nor did he, that the rebels already had possession of these works. Facing the regiment to the front, I ordered: "Forward—run; march!" We received no fire until we neared the breastworks, when the enemy who had possession of them, lying on the lower side, and who were completely surprised at our sudden arrival, rose up and fired a volley at us, and immediately retreated down the hill. This remarkable encounter did not last a minute. We lost two men, killed—both burned with the powder of the guns fired at them. The darkness and the suddenness of our arrival caused the enemy to fire wildly. We recaptured the breastworks.
>   Dawes would shout his orders to his men, calling out, "Down, men, watch sharp, keep your eyes peeled! Shoot low, shoot low, the hill is steep; quiet, now; steady!" After these orders and cautions, the men peered sharply into the woods to "let them have it" as they came up the hill against us.

The 6th Wisconsin entered the fray somewhere on the right of the 149th New York, possibly where Greene's and Kane's trenches met to form a right angle. Could the Confederates that Dawes encountered have been part of

Williams's Louisiana brigade, confirming the belief of many of the Cajuns that they had captured the works? Maybe, but highly doubtful. These Rebel troops seem more likely to be from the 37th or 23rd Virginia. The left of the 149th, if at all, had engaged the Louisiana boys and the 6th Wisconsin definitely arrived on the right of these New Yorkers. We know this because Colonel Dawes wrote about the events happening, almost simultaneously, on his right.

The danger was not over for the men of the 137th New York, as the enemy simply would not go away. Ireland had his men behind the traverse, holding on with every ounce of sinew and intestinal fortitude they could summon. Rather than sitting on the defensive and simply taking it, Ireland attacked! Captain Joseph Gregg, of Company I, led a small squad of men and "charged with the bayonet the enemy that were harassing us most, and fell, mortally wounded, leading and cheering on his men."

The gallant Gregg had fallen, but his efforts must have completely surprised his foe. Shot in the left shoulder and chest, he was carried to a field hospital in the rear. The surgeons amputated his left arm all the way to his shoulder, but they could not save him. At only twenty-six years old, Joseph H. Gregg, from Binghamton, New York, died the following day.

Relief came for those who still remained, as the 14th Brooklyn, those "Red-Legged Devils" with their bright red zouave pants, appeared somewhere near the 137th New York. No one seemed to be sure just who was who; the Brooklyn men said that "strange forms and voices" were seen and heard in their midst. Shadowy figures resembling a body of troops were moving and firing into their right flank. Colonel Edward Fowler, their commander in the regimental history of the 14th Brooklyn, explained:

> On arriving on the right, we received a fire from the inside of our lines, and, it then being quite dark I

Two views from the valley of the stone wall used by the 10th
Virginia. It is somewhere in this area where Sergeant John Cox of
the 14th Brooklyn did his scouting and where Captain Gregg of
the 137th New York led his bayonet charge.

was placed in a trying position to determine if we were being fired on by our friends, or if the enemy had penetrated inside of our line.

There was only one thing to do—a scouting party was needed to go forward in the dark and investigate. Two men supposedly volunteered for this hazardous duty; their names were McQuire and Sergeant John Cox (one of eight known men named John Cox in the great battle, none of whom are related to the author). Cox was a musician in Company I, and he seemed to always have been selected to perform the worst duties imaginable. At any rate, the two scouts went forward with trepidation "in the teeth of the flank fire." After many long and anxious moments, Cox returned, but McQuire was wounded and captured. Cox's reconnaissance revealed that indeed it was the enemy, the 10th Virginia. Fowler immediately ordered the men to open fire and the "Red-Legged Devils of Brooklyn" charged forward, causing "great disorder" and forcing the Rebels back. Greene's right flank was secure.

The 14th Brooklyn would now relieve the 137th New York, allowing Ireland and his men to fall back to the rear. The 147th New York would do the same for the 149th New York, with Greene's men retiring from the "pits" to clean their fouled weapons and replenish ammunition. It would be a system that the defenders of Culp's Hill would use the next day. Regiments would fight behind the breastworks and be relieved by others, so that the men could rest and, more importantly, maintain a constant supply of ammunition. During the course of the fighting on the evening of July 2, the Confederates had no such system. Their reserve ammunition supply was a mile or so to the rear! Lieutenant Randolph McKim would volunteer, with three other men, to resupply Steuart's brigade with bullets. He stated that he and the men were able to carry "three boxes of ammunition in blankets swung to rails." McKim received three of four close brushes with death on his return. He reported, "A ball grazed my shoulder as I was bringing the ammunition up Culp's Hill. Another went through my haversack and ripped the back off a New Testament I had in my pocket. Then the piece of shell rebounded from a tree and struck me in the back." Desperate for ammunition, the efforts of McKim and his crew, though courageous, could hardly have satisfied the need.

The darkness made the movement of reinforcements to Greene's front extremely difficult. The Eleventh Corps regiments also received a flurry of contradictory orders. Lieutenant Colonel Adolphus Dobke, commander of the 45th New York reported:

> For a mile through the complete darkness in the woods this regiment pushed up to the stone fence through an incessant shower of bullets, and shared well in the defense of this position. It is to be mentioned that while the regiment marched in the darkness through the woods, under guide of a staff officer, the march was considerably delayed by a number of general staff officers, each exerting himself to give his orders, and so, by movements, coun-

A view of some of the rough terrain over which Steuart's men had to advance in the darkness.

termovements, halts &c., some time elapsed before the regiment found itself in the right place behind the fence.

At some point during this fighting a detachment of the 157th New York came to Ireland's relief, or somewhere to the right, though the assistance they provided must have been brief and limited. During their encounter with the Confederates, the color-bearer of the 157th New York, George H. Davis, fell wounded. Sergeant Thomas J. Betterton of Company A, 37th Virginia, recovered "a stand of colors and was severely wounded." It is presumed, but not entirely clear, that the colors Sergeant Betterton retrieved were those of the 157th New York.

The major fighting on Culp's Hill ended at about 10:00 P.M., although periodically, shots and sporadic volleys would be fired at noises or movements made in the dark. Captain Collins wrote,

> the cessation of hostilities for the night, which occurred by degrees and by common consent, it was found that eighty rounds of cartridge had been expended to the man.

Greene's line had held and the Army of the Potomac was saved from the dire consequences of a possible defeat.

During the night the remainder of the Twelfth Corps returned to their former positions, only to find their places sometimes filled with Confederate troops. Some units like the 111th Pennsylvania simply walked into their former position, where the breastworks formed a right angle just above the saddle area, and received a point-blank fire coming out of total darkness. Other Union units, not entirely convinced that the Confederates could have taken the breastworks, sent out scouts to reconnoiter. Many of these men would simply walk right into the enemy's lines. The 123rd New York sent out skirmishers upon their return to the hill to investigate their front. The skirmishers quickly came under fire from the Rebels who now occupied their former position. Naturally, these skirmishers high-tailed it for the rear and safety, only to come under the fire of the 145th New York, who mistook them for Confederates.

The shooting would last all through the night, but soon both sides settled down and formed new battle lines to await the heavy fighting to follow. The Union line now extended, virtually west, from the traverse, before heading due south, facing Pardee Field. Artillery and infantry units also covered the Baltimore Pike and then the line turned due east, stretching to Rock Creek.

On the Confederate right, Jones's brigade formed a line considerably further back than the other brigades in the division. Lieutenant Colonel Salyer of the 50th Virginia reported, beginning with an all-too-familiar saying, of where their new line was formed:

> It may be well to state here that when we fell back we carried every one of our killed and wounded with us to the base of the hill. This night we slept at the base of the hill, about 300 yards from the enemy's lines.

Williams's Louisiana brigade was able to maintain a position about 100 to 150 yards from Greene's main line, but it was still hazardous. W. G. Loyd of the 2nd Louisiana found that a good stretch of the legs could be a dangerous move. Loyd wrote:

> An order was passed along our line to cease firing and lie down. We did so, securing protection behind the numerous rocks to be found on the side of the mountain. Shortly afterwards, in my efforts to "hug the ground," not being behind a very large rock, I threw my legs our farther than necessary,

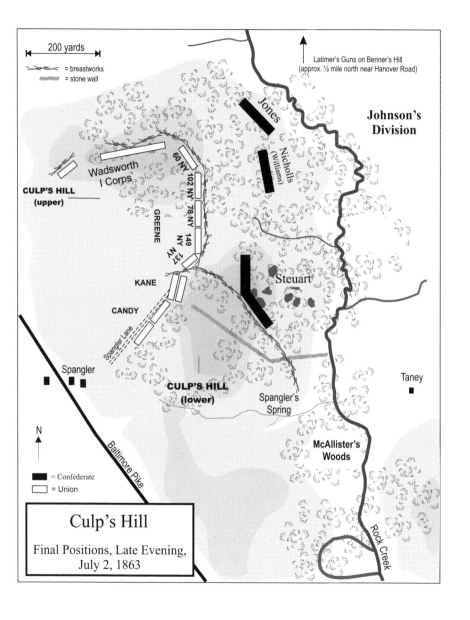

200 yards

≈≈≈ = breastworks
≈≈≈ = stone wall

Latimer's Guns on Benner's Hill
(approx. ½ mile north near Hanover Road)

Jones

Nicholls
(Williams)

Johnson's
Division

Wadsworth
I Corps

60 NY
102 NY
78 NY
149 NY
137 NY

CULP'S HILL
(upper)

GREENE

Steuart

KANE

CANDY

Spangler Lane

Spangler

CULP'S HILL
(lower)

Spangler's
Spring

Taney

N

McAllister's
Woods

= Confederate
= Union

Baltimore Pike

Rock Creek

Culp's Hill

Final Positions, Late Evening,
July 2, 1863

> when a minie ball from the enemy on our right struck my right leg below the knee.

Loyd would be helped by his mates and carried 200 yards to the rear near Rock Creek. The following day after the fighting ended, no one was able to help him and he was captured. He was sent to David's Island, on Long Island Sound, where a hospital was located to assist wounded prisoners. Two months later, he was exchanged and served out the war.

The Confederate left remained in part of the trenches they had captured that evening. Their attack was not a total failure, as has been mentioned, because they had gained a foothold on the Union right flank. Confident that his men could do more damage, even possibly collapsing this flank, Ewell brought in reinforcements during the night. He essentially doubled his strength on the hill and waited for daylight. Around midnight, the Stonewall Brigade finally rejoined Johnson's division, having completed its duties at Brinkerhoff's Ridge.

The casualties for the fighting on Culp's Hill are hard to assess because there would be seven hours of continuous combat the next day. All casualty reports took into account both days of the fighting. Some of the Confederate brigades did not even list casualties. Johnson's division would suffer 30.1 percent casualties over the two days, with 373 killed, 1,150 wounded, and 413 missing. Some Confederates thought the fighting was significant enough to earn the sobriquet of the "valley of death." Thus, the original "valley of death" was in the Culp's Hill area, not between the Devil's Den and Little Round Top.

Greene's brigade had casualties of 21.3 percent, with 67 killed, 212 wounded, and 24 missing. Reading over the listings of the men killed on July 2, it is remarkable to note that almost all of the men died from gunshots to the head and neck. This means that Greene's breastworks did their job and saved countless lives. Another interesting fact concerning casualties is that the 20th Maine on Little Round Top suffered a loss of 32.4 percent. Conversely, the 137th New York, on the right flank, suffered exactly the same, 32.4 percent casualties. Colonel Ireland and his men, however, suffered more total casualties with 40 killed, 87 wounded, and 10 missing, for a total of 137 out of 423 engaged. The 20th Maine, by comparison, had 29 killed, 91 wounded, and 5 missing, for a total of 125 out of 386.

Lieutenant Randolph H. McKim claimed an accomplishment that no other man could do. He wrote:

> I have sometimes remarked that I thought I performed an exploit at Gettysburg that none of them could match. "What is that?" "Why," said I, "I went sound asleep in the very midst of the heaviest firing, lying in the Federal breastworks!" And I did, in very deed and truth.

McKim said that he had been up for six straight days, marching all those miles and that he suffered from "such utter exhaustion" that he had no fear of danger.

## Conclusion

The battle for Culp's Hill on the evening of July 2, 1863, was unique, defying most of the established rules for Civil War combat. The fighting took place at night, a relative rarity in that era. Civil War soldiers did not normally fight in the darkness, to be overly simplistic, because it was too hard to see. It was too easy to get lost and too easy to fire on your friends, never mind trying to locate the enemy. There were more incidents of friendly fire at Culp's Hill on the evening of July 2 than anywhere else at Gettysburg.

The fact that Greene's men fought behind breastworks was another reason that the action was unusual. Building entrenchments and then remaining behind them was not a concept that became popular until later in the Civil War. The trenches around Petersburg, Virginia, are a good example of how the war changed and how important fortifications became. Culp's Hill was an aberration and a precursor of things to come.

As has been discussed, General Ewell's performance at Gettysburg was just as good and just as bad as his colleagues in the Army of Northern Virginia. For far too long, historians have criticized his actions in an attempt to explain away the Confederate defeat at Gettysburg. His apparent hesitation to attack Cemetery Hill has almost overshadowed the importance of Culp's Hill on July 1 in the equation.

Ewell's attack on Culp's Hill on July 2, rather than being "late" and not "simultaneous" with Longstreet's main assault, was extremely aggressive. He saw an opportunity that, in the end, had very little to do with Longstreet's attack. He launched a "real attack" because he felt the enemy in his front had presented an opening and he decided to achieve the initiative. As stated, Ewell was the only corps commander in the Confederate army to breech the "fish hook" and hold it. His attack achieved a partial success. The actions of the following day, however, are a different matter.

**Sketch from a photograph of General Greene**

150

Why is General Greene's performance at Gettysburg so overlooked? The question is not too hard to answer. Briefly, some of the reasons for this oversight will be explained.

General Greene and his men were forgotten almost immediately! Meade failed to mention them in his Official Report of the battle. He simply stated that during the assault on the left

> portions of the Twelfth Corps were sent as re-enforcements. During their absence, the line on the extreme right was held by a very much reduced force. This was taken advantage of by the enemy, who, during the absence of Geary's division of the Twelfth Corps, advanced and occupied a part of his line.

Meade unknowingly added salt to the wound by mistakenly writing in his first report that Lockwood's brigade was under the command of the First Corps. This infuriated the men of the Twelfth Corps, believing that Meade had purposefully overlooked them. General Williams wrote:

> certain errors and omissions in Major General Meade's official report of that battle, which I think do much injustice to some portions of this corps.

Meade defended himself against the barrage of criticisms in a letter, written on February 25, 1864. In it he stated that he regretted any injustices done in his Official Report regarding the conduct of the Twelfth Corps. He also said that his report relied heavily on the information from the reports of his corps commanders. An important factor in the dispute was that the Twelfth Corps left the Army of the Potomac after Gettysburg, merging with the Eleventh Corps and joining the Army of the Cumberland in Tennessee. In addition, Slocum had to wait for the report of General Ruger, who was sent to New York City to quell the draft riots there. All this caused Slocum to be the last corps commander to send Meade his report. Meade, therefore, turned the criticisms around in his letter and blamed the officers of the Twelfth Corps for any omissions or errors. Meade stated that his report was also just a brief statement and that if he had been made aware of Greene's actions, he would have given it special mention. That same day, February 25, 1864, Meade wrote another letter to General in Chief Henry Halleck, in Washington, with an amendment to his Official Report of February 1864:

> During the heavy assaults upon our extreme left, the First Division and Lockwood's brigade, of the Twelfth Corps, were sent as re-inforcements, as already reported. Two brigades of Geary's division (Second, of this corps) were also detached for the same purpose, but did not arrive at the scene of action, owing to having mistaken the road.

Meade believed that he had rectified the hostilities with the men of the Twelfth Corps. He also did one more thing. In March 1864 he wrote a letter to General Greene and attached his amended report. He apologized to Greene for any injustice that may have been done and said that had he known, he would have mentioned the services that Greene and his men performed.

Other factors have contributed to obscure Greene's defense of Culp's Hill. One of them is that the fighting took place at night and Culp's Hill was somewhat isolated from the view of Union troops along Cemetery Ridge. Adding to this is the fact that the hill was heavily wooded, which also decreased visibility. Secondly, Greene was not the kind of man, as many others in the army were, to boast or exaggerate his contributions to the victory. Greene was the type that quietly went about his business and did his duty.

Another important factor why Greene's performance remains relatively unnoticed is that the numbers of troops engaged, including casualties, were comparatively low. Longstreet's assault on the south part of the battlefield involved tremendous numbers and great loss of life. The fighting at Culp's Hill seems small by comparison, but the importance was no less. Also, Greene's men were not completely wiped out, killed down to the last man in a desperate attempt to hold the hill. They simply held their position, with few casualties, and blasted the enemy. It does not seem as heroic as the stand of the 16th Maine on the first day or the charge of the 1st Minnesota on the second. Though, most of us would surely agree, that if we had to fight at Gettysburg, wouldn't we rather be under Greene's command? Is it not the ideal role of a commander to suffer as few casualties as possible, while inflicting the maximum amount on the enemy? This is exactly what General Greene did.

Brigadier General George Sears Greene and his men, with special recognition to Colonel David Ireland, won the battle of Gettysburg on the evening of July 2, 1863, at Culp's Hill. The heroic defense of the right flank by Greene and his men saved Major General George G. Meade from his biggest mistake of the battle, the consequences of which would have been disaster. Greene's defense not only secured the right flank, but also insured the safety of Cemetery Hill and the Baltimore Pike. The loss of Culp's Hill would have caused a complete and total collapse of the Army of the Potomac's position at Gettysburg. The possible loss of that army's position, due to a failure to maintain control of Culp's Hill, could have lost the army's ammunition trains and artillery reserve, not to mention its best line of retreat. Summarily, without Greene's gallant and bold stand, the battle of Gettysburg would have been more than a defeat for Union arms, but rather a horrific catastrophe. These observations, however, are needless, because Greene and his men did their duty.

The facts of the case may crush some preconceived notions for those who even sympathize with General

Greene. When the officers of the Second Division of the Twelfth Corps had their discussion about breastworks, early in the morning upon arrival at Culp's Hill, it is not clear who ordered their construction. Greene did not build the first trenches on the hill, therefore, it was not his idea. He did, however, take advantage of them. It is certain, however, that he had the foresight to build the traverse. When the Twelfth Corps was ordered to vacate the hill and move to the threatened left flank, it is not clear who ordered Greene to stay. It is possible that it was Greene's own decision, as the Confederate attack was just developing in his front, but it is not clear.

What is left then to praise Greene, if he did not do all these things? As the imminent historian John Keegan relates, there is one thing a general on a battlefield can not calculate; the question of if his men will "stand." Greene's men stood. They stood because he trained them to do so. They made a stand, because Greene was standing, and he refused to be moved. Greene led with the greatest quality of a leader, by his actions. He was a fearless warrior and a quiet patriot. His example screamed out to them, "Be a soldier, fight and do not give an inch," but he never uttered the words. He did not have to; he just stood silently and they knew. If we listen to the comments of the men that served under him we hear this clearly.

Colonel Abel Godard wrote in his Official Report:

> All the commands were received by the men coolly, and instantly obeyed, more especially the orders "commence firing" and "cease firing."

Captain Lewis R. Stegman, in his dedication speech for the Greene Monument at Gettysburg, on September 27, 1907, said:

> The blaze of fire which lighted up the darkness in the valley, the desperate charging yell and halloa of

General Greene's grave in Apponaug, Rhode Island. A bronze plaque with a sword above it was once affixed to the rock, from Culp's Hill, that marks his headstone. Thieves, however, removed the plaque in hopes of financial gain. Luckily, Rhode Island authorities were able to arrest the villains and recover the plaque, which is now on display in the Warwick City Hall. At present, the Greene family cemetery is in deplorable condition, despite the best efforts of many citizens. Forgotten in life, George Sears Greene is tragically also forgotten in death.

the Confederate troops, convinced the boys of Greene's Brigade that an immediate engagement was on. They faced the emergency as became good soldiers, their volleys ringing in fierce reply to the Confederate offense. They battled with the determination that makes success. There were no heroics on the line except in the stern duty well done.

Greene, however, has been forgotten, his deeds lost in the running of time. Other men have risen up and taken all the acclaim that there is to give. Men like Chamberlain, Reynolds, and Hancock. Is there not any recognition left for the forgotten hero of Culp's Hill? At Gettysburg you will find no T-shirts or hats that honor old "Pop"—that market is full. We can remember Greene like he lived: quietly and unassuming. We, too, can be satisfied that the man did all he could do and he did it very well.

# TOURING THE FIELD

THIS TOUR IS STRAIGHTFORWARD and should be easy to follow. Before beginning, let me stress safety. The rocks on Culp's Hill are extremely slippery and treacherous, even when not wet. Moisture makes them doubly dangerous. A major portion of the tour may require walking over some rough ground, so watch your step. While driving, always obey the posted speed limits. For those who do not feel the necessity to step over rocks, walk over very uneven ground, or up steep inclines, I have offered options to view the battle scenes from key spots where you can easily imagine the struggle.

I have not included Brinkerhoff's Ridge in this tour because it involves some dangerous driving. Those who wish to examine the ground there can merely drive east on Route 116, the Hanover Road, and turn left on Hoffman Road. Otherwise, the tour that is included here should suffice.

From the Visitor Center parking lot, go left. You are on Cemetery Hill on the Taneytown Road. Driving down the hill, go right at the traffic light. At the next traffic light bear left onto Baltimore Street. Take your very next right, which is Lefever Street. You are driving in the school district of Gettysburg, so please obey the school speed limit of 15 miles per hour.

At the next stop sign, go left (going right would take you to Culp's Hill, but we are not going there yet). At the next stop sign, go right and follow this road, East Middle Street. It will bear left and you will reach a stop sign. Go right onto Hanover Road, Route 116.

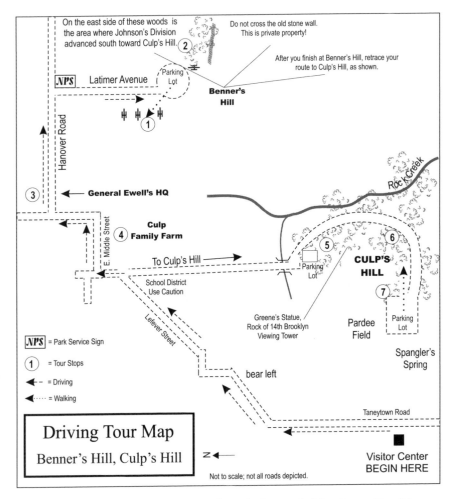

On the east side of these woods is the area where Johnson's Division advanced south toward Culp's Hill.

Do not cross the old stone wall. This is private property!

After you finish at Benner's Hill, retrace your route to Culp's Hill, as shown.

**NPS** Latimer Avenue

Parking Lot

**Benner's Hill**

Hanover Road

3

**General Ewell's HQ**

E. Middle Street

**Culp Family Farm** 4

To Culp's Hill →

School District Use Caution

Rock Creek

Parking Lot 5

**CULP'S HILL**

6

7 Parking Lot

Lefever Street

Greene's Statue, Rock of 14th Brooklyn Viewing Tower

Pardee Field

Spangler's Spring

bear left

Taneytown Road

**NPS** = Park Service Sign

1 = Tour Stops

= Driving

= Walking

# Driving Tour Map

Benner's Hill, Culp's Hill

N ←

Not to scale; not all roads depicted.

Visitor Center **BEGIN HERE**

The National Park Service has designated this site as Ewell's headquarters during the battle and it is marked by the upright cannon barrel. You cannot park on this side of the street, so if you wish to look around or take a picture, you will need to do it on our return trip. You may park on the other side of the street, facing the opposite direction.

Less than a half-mile ahead, at the top of the hill, take a right in front of the brown National Park Service sign. You are on Benner's Hill, the Confederate artillery position for their attack on the Union right flank. Drive to the end of the road (it's called Latimer Avenue) to the roundabout. Park the car on the loop, on the right side of the road. Walk to the guns lined up on your left. Look in the direction that they are facing. You can see a green water tower in the distance. This water tower is on Cemetery Hill and is a good landmark to remind you of your location on the field. Cemetery Hill, of course, is the Union artillery position. Culp's Hill is to the left of Cemetery Hill. You also have an excellent view of the town of Gettysburg.

The text describes the action that took place on this spot. If you wish you can walk the gun line and read the markers, which explain where the different batteries were located during the fight. You will also notice that there are more guns on the other side of the Hanover Road. It is not recommended that you cross the road, but use extreme caution if you decide to do so. The speed limit on this section of the Hanover Road is 45 mph and traffic, of course, is sometimes moving faster than that.

If you look behind the guns and slightly to your left, you will see the stone house of the Daniel Lady farm, which is private property. The Confederate infantry of Johnson's division, excluding the skirmishers, were in this general area, lined up on the north or opposite side of the Hanover Road.

**The Daniel Lady Farm on the Hanover Road.**

Walk back to the loop where your car is parked and walk to the two rifled (black) guns, pointed in a somewhat different direction than the rest of Major Latimer's guns. These two guns were part of Raines's or Lee's battery from Virginia. Walk to the left of these two guns, slightly into the woods, and up to the low (almost non-existent) stone wall at the edge of the woods. As always, watch out for poison ivy. (Do not walk over the stone wall—this is private property, as the many signs indicate; please be respectful.)

There should be a farm on your left and a sloping field in your front. This is the area where the skirmishers fought during the day. It also is the location of the advance of the Confederates of Johnson's division for their attack on Culp's Hill. Culp's Hill is the wooded heights on your right. If you look closely you can see the observation tower poking out above the trees. The wooded hill on your left is Wolf's Hill, the "left-wing" of Steuart's brigade advanced slightly over its base.

We will now drive to Culp's Hill, retracing the route we just used. Drive to the end of Latimer Avenue and take a left. Be very careful of oncoming traffic, especially on your right. Drive past the bridge over Rock Creek and take a left by Ewell's headquarters (the upright cannon barrel). You may want to park immedi-

**The Culp Family Farm.**

**A view of the ground where the Confederates advanced to attack Culp's Hill. Culp's Hill is located in the right center background, much more heavily wooded today than in 1863.**

ately on your right to take a picture or look around at this spot. Continuing on, bear right on East Middle Street (passing the stop sign) and go straight. You will pass the red barn and stone house of the Culp Farm on your left. If you wish to stop, park on the right side of the road and walk across the street.

Moving on, take a left at the stop sign and go straight ahead, through the wooden gate. You are on the road to Culp's Hill, called East Confederate Avenue, and on National Park property. This is a one-way road. The Gettysburg Middle School should be on your right. On your left, you will see stone walls and plank-and-rail fences. Drive until you cross over the small bridge and very carefully pull over and park on the right. Be careful because the ground can sometimes be very wet and muddy. You should see Jones's brigade marker on the left side of the road. (There is a marker for every brigade of Johnson's division along this route.) On your right is the steepest slope of Culp's Hill and this is where Jones's Virginians assaulted Greene's line. For those who are extremely ambitious and rugged, there is a small path that leads up the hill. Walk to where the woods form a right angle, which should be easily visible. It is a very tough climb and is not advised for those who are physically unable to handle such stress. Imagine being a Confederate soldier trying to scale this hill under fire!

Progressing forward, drive straight ahead. All along this road is where Lieutenant Colonel Redington and his skirmishers tried to slow down the Confederate advance. On your left, through the woods, is Rock Creek, which was a formidable obstacle for the Rebels to cross. If you wish you can park anywhere on this road, preferably somewhere on the left where it is sometimes semi-paved, otherwise park on the right. Walk through the woods on your left to get a view of Rock Creek. If you do not wish to fight briers and rocks, keep driving.

(Anytime you are on the battlefield you should try to park in designated parking spaces; if not, use good judgment and if you really want to stop, always park on the right. In some places along East Confederate Avenue, the road has semi-paved, mostly gravel, pull-offs on the left. Use common sense and be careful of muddy ground. By all means, do whatever a Park Ranger instructs—they are the final authority on all matters concerning driving and parking on the battlefield.)

Drive till you reach a stop sign and go right, parking in the designated spaces provided there. To your front are rocks and trees

**Spangler's Spring.**

162

and very slightly to your left, the ground rises and you will see monuments. To your back left is the legendary Spangler's Spring, where it is said that on the night of July 2 Confederate and Union soldiers had an unspoken cease-fire agreement and shared water. It is my opinion that this anecdote is, in fact, myth. The struggle for the possession of the hill was too deadly and confusing to think soldiers would do this; but the legend persists.

If you want to leave your vehicle here, walk toward the stop sign where you just turned. Look to your left for the stone wall in the woods, on the opposite side of the road. Now do an about face and look up just to the right of Spangler's Spring and try to find the stone wall again. You are standing in the location where Steuart's brigade attacked.

From the parking area by Spangler's Spring, back out of your parking place and head up the hill, going right. You are ascending the smaller of the two hills in the Culp's Hill complex.

**The monument to the 1st Maryland Infantry CSA, renamed the 2nd Maryland Infantry. This was the first Confederate regimental monument placed on the battlefield in 1886.**

Looking to your right you may be able to see the Union trench-line. As you pass by the rocks and monuments scattered along the hill, you will soon reach the summit of the smaller hill. Pull off on your right by the granite monument with a large, look-alike cannon ball on its top. This is the 2nd Maryland (Confederate) Infantry monument. You'll notice that it sits directly in the Union trench line. Look closely at its base and you will notice that in the fine print, above where it says 2nd Maryland, there is an inscription that reads: "1st MD changed to 2nd MD." This is because, on Culp's Hill, Maryland faced Maryland. Union troops from Maryland, who called themselves the "1st," would not allow Confederate troops the same designation. Hence, the Confederate Veterans from Maryland were forced to change from the 1st to the 2nd. Another interesting point of trivia is that this was the first Confederate Regimental monument placed on the battlefield.

You are on the summit of the smaller hill. It is somewhere in this area or slightly down the hill on the way you just traveled where the 1st Maryland and 23rd Virginia gained the flank of the 137th New York.

Look in the opposite direction, down the hill, and you will see the valley or "saddle" between the two hills. Look off to your left and through the trees and locate the stone wall. This is the stone wall the 10th Virginia used to guide itself as they advanced.

Drive the curvy road down to the valley and pull off on the right where it is semi-paved with gravel. You are now in the "saddle" area.

We can now divide the tour up between "walkers" and "drivers." If you wish to do some walking, you will need to drive first. If you wish to do a more casual tour with more driving, you will need to walk first and then drive.

Walkers should continue driving, staying to the right, until you reach the top of the larger hill, by General Greene's statue. Leave your vehicle and walk straight down the hill from Greene's statue. You will pass the 60th New York monument and see a smaller plaque monument a little further down the hill. This is the marker for Company I of the 60th New York, and also the area where Jones's Virginians attacked the 60th New York.

Drivers who wish a more casual tour, leave your car parked and walk up the opposite hill from the one you were just on, to the rock that has the plaque attached on its front. This rock is a monument to the 14th Brooklyn and is also the location of General Greene's traverse.

Walkers should continue moving to your right, following the Union trenchline. In fact, walkers should continue moving to their right, just as Greene's men shifted as the Confederate attack began. Eventually, you will end up where we left the drivers off, by the rock with the plaque in its front, for the 14th Brooklyn. As you pass the small flank markers, off to your left you will see a larger boulder, bigger even than a mini-van. This rock can be clearly seen in the famous illustration by Edwin Forbes. You will also pass by two Union monuments on your right. Keep walking till you are in front of the 78th and 102nd New York monument. This is where Williams's brigade assaulted Greene's line.

**The Confederates attacking Culp's Hill in this painting by Edwin Forbes. The boulders depicted in the painting are easily identifiable on Culp's Hill today.**

**A modern view of one of the boulders as seen in the Forbes painting.**

**Drivers:** The battle action occurred off on your left.

**Walkers:** Continue moving to the right, following the trench. Walk to the front of the 149th New York monument. You may need to walk out of the trench and look on the front of the monument to find the right one. Placing yourself anywhere in this area, though, is fine. The front of the 149th New York monument is worth looking for, as the bas relief on its front depicts Sergeant Lilly mending the regiments flag during the fight.

**The monument to the 149th New York Infantry from a Confederate perspective, looking up to the Union trenchline.**

**Drivers:** You are getting closer to the action , still on your left.

**Walkers:** You should now proceed to where we left off the drivers, at the rock monument of the 14th Brooklyn. Look across the saddle area, to the top of the crest of the smaller hill. The fighting retreat and the "refusing" of the line by the 137th New York happened in front of you. Meanwhile, it should be remembered that the Confederates continued their attacks on your left front, storming Greene's breastworks. To your right is where the 71st Pennsylvania moved into the saddle area, while the 6th Wisconsin gained the Union trenches somewhere to your left. The 14th Brooklyn, of course, will enter the fight about where you are standing.

The drivers can now re-enter their vehicles, while the walkers can advance back up the hill to their cars. The walkers, however, should walk alongside the road this time and not along the trenches. The walkers can now follow the tour of the drivers; you'll just have to walk this portion of the tour.

Drive up the main hill, and stay to the right. Just around that first curve, as you are ascending the hill, not far from the 14th Brooklyn's rock, pull over to the right. Find the monument with the star on top and "137" written in it. This is the monument for

**Monument to the 137th New York. Notice the rocky ground on which the monument stands.**

**General Greene keeps a constant vigil on the crest of Culp's Hill. The Observation Tower is in the background.**

the 137th New York. Ironically, they suffered 137 casualties in the battle, which is inscribed on their monument.

When you are done examining the 137th's monument, drive a very short distance and again pull over. There are two more monuments placed very close together on your right. The one on the left is the monument for 149th New York and the bas relief on its front shows Sergeant Lilly mending the regiment's flag, under fire.

When you are done looking at this monument, drive ahead a very short distance and pull off to the right in front of the monument with the soldier firing his rifled musket behind a stone wall. This is the monument for the 78th and 102nd New York and gives us an excellent flavor of how the men in Greene's brigade fought on Culp's Hill. Look very closely at this monument and see if you can find the optical illusion of the lion.

Return to your vehicle and continue driving, bearing to the right, till you reach the crest of the main hill. Park in the designated parking spaces. Here is the statue of General Greene, pointing down the hill, leading his men in the fight. If you wish you can walk straight down the hill from the General's statue to the 60th New York monument. Moving further down the hill, you will find the small plaque of Company I of the 60th New

**Marker for the 6th Wisconsin in the Iron Brigade trenches, at a right angle to Greene's line.**

York, commanded by Captain Jesse Jones, who wore the breast-plates during the fighting. Use good judgment about walking down the hill—it can be steeper than it looks and if you wish, you can still see these monuments simply by standing in front of Greene's statue.

Those who so desire can walk the stairs to the top of the observation tower, which gives an excellent view of the town of Gettysburg and the battlefield.

Re-enter your vehicle and make the turn around the observation tower. As you go around this curve you will see the monument to the 7th Indiana, the boys from Company B of this regiment spoiled Johnson's reconnaissance on the night of July 1.

As you drive down the hill, those who would like to see the trenches of the Iron Brigade can pull over to the right, about 100 to 150 yards down the hill from the observation tower. Walk into the woods on your right. There are markers in the woods that designate the position of the different regiments of the Iron Brigade. See if you can find them.

Driving down the hill, the trees will soon clear a little on your right and you will be able to see the trenches of the Iron Brigade. Just before you reach Major General Henry Slocum's monument (on your left), there will be a small marker on your right, in the old trenches. This is a marker for the 24th Michigan regiment of the Iron Brigade. You can pull over, again on the right, just past this small marker. You are now on Stevens's Knoll, the rise of ground that connects Cemetery Hill with Culp's Hill. The hill off in the distance, somewhat facing the view of your windshield, is Cemetery Hill. On the crest of the heights of the knoll, on your left, you can see General Slocum, commander of the Twelfth Corps, upon his horse. Look at the ground in the direction that he is facing. This is the terrain the Confederates advanced over to attack both Cemetery Hill on your left and Culp's Hill on your right.

As you continue driving, go left, until you reach the stop sign, and turn left. You are now on the Baltimore Pike. Drive about a half mile and turn right, onto Hunt Avenue. Follow this road till it ends, being very careful around the turn and going over the small, one lane bridge. You have the right of way on the bridge, but not all motorists are aware of this, nor do they respect it! As you reach the stop sign, the small white house with the white picket fence was General Meade's headquarters during the battle. Go right. When you reach the top of the hill you are at the Visitor's Center.

If you want to examine the Union artillery position on East Cemetery Hill, instead of ending the tour at the Visitor's Center, continue driving straight ahead, just like when we began the tour. Take a right at the traffic light at the bottom of the hill. Just off to your right, by the way, is the "Friend to Friend" monument, dedicated to the freemasons, but pay attention to your driving! At the next traffic light, by the gas station, take a very hard and sharp right. As you gain the top of the hill (Cemetery Hill), pull over, and park along the street. You will have to put some coins in the parking meter. Be very careful and cross the street. You are now at the artillery position for the Union army, commanded by Colonel Wainwright, that opposed Major Latimer's guns on Benner's Hill.

It should be easy for you to return to the Visitor's Center from this location, as you are back on the Baltimore Pike.

# BIBLIOGRAPHY

Bandy, Ken, and Freeland, Florence, The Gettysburg Papers, 2 volumes, Morningside Bookshop, 1986.

Bates, Samuel P., *History of the Pennsylvania Volunteers, 1861–1865,* 5 volumes, Harrisburg, 1869–1871.

Blair, William Alan, and Wiley, Bell Irvin, editors, *A Politician Goes To War: The Civil War Letters of John White Geary,* Pennsylvania State University, 1995.

Brown, Edmund R., *History of Twenty-seventh Indiana Volunteer Infantry,* Monticello, 1899.

Burrows, Edwin G., and Wallace, Mike, *Gotham: A History of New York City to 1898*, Oxford University Press, 1999.

Busey, John W., *These Honored Dead: The Union Casualties at Gettysburg,* Longstreet House, 1996.

Busey, John W., and Martin, David G., *Regimental Strengths and Losses at Gettysburg*, Longstreet House, 1986.

Casler, John O., *Four Years with the Stonewall Brigade*, Morningside Bookshop, 1994.

Cave, Alfred A., *The Pequot War*, The University of Massachusetts Press, 1996.

Clark, Walter, editor, *Histories of the Several Regiments and Battalions from North Carolina in the Great War, 1861–65,* 5 volumes, Raleigh: State of North Carolina, 1901.

Coddington, Edwin B., *The Gettysburg Campaign: A Study in Command*, Charles Scribner's Sons, 1968.

Coggins, Jack, *Arms & Equipment of the Civil War*, The Fairfax Press, 1983 edition.

Collins, George K., *Memories of the 149ᵗʰ Regiment, New York Volunteer Infantry*, Reprinted by Edmonston Publishing, Inc., 1995.

Crute, Joseph H. Jr., *Units of the Confederate States Army*, Reprinted by Olde Soldier Books, Inc., 1987.

D'Amato, Donald A., *The Walking Tour of Historic Apponaug Village*, Warwick Economic Development Department Tourism Office, 1998.

Danforth, William, Letters, Minnesota Historical Society.

Dawes, Rufus R., Service with the Sixth Wisconsin Volunteers. Marietta, Ohio, 1890.

Douglas, Henry Kyd, *I Rode with Stonewall*, University of North Carolina Press, 1940.

Dowdey, Clifford, *Death of a Nation: The Story of Lee and His Men at Gettysburg*, reprinted by Butternut and Blue, 1992.

Dowdey, Clifford, and Manarin, Louis H., *The Wartime Papers of Robert E. Lee*, Da Capo Press, Inc., 1961.

Downey, Fairfax, *The Guns at Gettysburg*, reprinted by Olde Soldier Books Inc., 1987.

Early, Jubal A., *Narrative of the War Between the States*, Da Capo Press, reprinted 1989.

Eddy, Richard, *History of the Sixtieth Regiment, New York State Volunteers*, Philadelphia: Cressy and Markley Printing, 1864.

Elmore, Thomas L., *Courage Against the Trenches: The Attack and Repulse of Steuart's Brigade on Culp's Hill*, Gettysburg Magazine, July 1992.

Faust, Patricia L., editor, *Historical Times Illustrated: Encyclopedia of the Civil War*, Harper & Row, 1986.

Fennell, Charles C., *Attack and Defense of Culp's Hill: Greene and His Men at Gettysburg*, Dissertation, University of West Virginia, 1992.

———. *Battle for the Barb: The Attack and Defense of Culp's Hill on July 2, 1863*, Friends of the National Park of Gettysburg, Inc., 2001.

Fleming, Thomas, *The Man from Monticello: An Intimate Life of Thomas Jefferson*, William Morrow and Company, Inc., New York, 1969.

Fox, William F., editor, New York Monuments Commission, *Final Report on the Battlefield of Gettysburg*, 3 volumes, by Fox, William F., Albany, J. B. Lyon Company, 1902.

———. New York Monuments Commission, *Greene and his New York Troops at Gettysburg*, Albany, J .B. Lyon Company, 1909.

Frassanito, William A., *Gettysburg: A Journey in Time*, Thomas Publications, 1975.

———. *Early Photography at Gettysburg*, Thomas Publications, 1995.

Fredericksburg National Military Park Files

    Camden, Edward D., Letters

    King, John R., *My Experience In The Confederate Army and in Northern Prisons*, United Daughters of Confederacy, 1917.

    Rawlings, Nathan J., *War Time Stories. . . Being. . . Thrilling Experiences and Adventures of Captain Nathan J. Rawlings, During the War 1861–65*, McCauley, Texas, September, 1909.

Freeman, Douglas Southall, *Lee Lieutenants*, 3 volumes, New York: Charles Scribner's Sons, 1949–1951.

———. *R. E. Lee: A Biography*, 4 volumes, New York: Charles Scribner's Sons, 1934–1935.

Fremantle, Arthur J. L., *Three Months in the Southern States*, University of Nebraska Press, A Bison Book, 1991.

Gettysburg National Military Park Vertical Files

    Coon, Steuben H., Letter

    Hyde, James S., Diary

    Jeffers, Ira S., Letters

    Jones, Benjamin Anderson, Letters

    Snakenberg, W. P., Memoirs

    Zable, David, Letters

Goldsborough, W. W., *The Maryland Line in the Confederate Army*, Reprinted by Olde Soldier Books, Inc., 1987.

Gordon, John B., *Reminiscences of the Civil War*, reprinted Time-Life Books Inc., 1981.

Griffith, Paddy, *Battle Tactics of the Civil War*, Yale University Press, 1989.

Hebert, Walter H., *Fighting Joe Hooker*, The Bobbs-Merrill Company, 1944, reprinted by Olde Soldier Books, Inc.

Johnson, Robert Underwood, and Buel, Clarence Clough, editors, *Battles and Leaders of the Civil War*, 4 volumes, New York: Century Company, 1884–1889, reprinted New York, Thomas Yoseloff, 1956.

Jorgensen, Jay, *Joseph W. Latimer, The "Boy Major," at Gettysburg*, Gettysburg Magazine, January 1994.

———. *Holding the Right: The 137th New York Regiment at Gettysburg*, Gettysburg Magazine, July 1996.

Keegan, John, *The Face of Battle*, Penguin Books, 1976.

Ladd, David L., and Ladd, Audrey J., editors, *The Bachelder Papers: Gettysburg in Their Own Words*, 3 volumes, Morningside Bookshop, 1994.

Lippincott, George E., *The Exchange of Rooney Lee*, Civil War Times Illustrated, June 1962.

Livy, *The War with Hannibal*, Penguin Books, 1965.

Lloyd, W. G., *Second Louisiana at Gettysburg*, Confederate Veteran 6 (September 1898): 417.

McKim, Randolph H., *A Soldier's Recollections*, Longmans, Green, and Co., 1910.

Meade, George G. Jr., *The Life and Letters of George Gordon Meade*, New York: Charles Scribner's Sons, 1913, reprinted Butternut and Blue, 1994.

Motts, Wayne E., *To Gain a Second Star: The Forgotten George S. Greene*, Gettysburg Magazine, July 1990.

Murfin, James V., *The Gleam of Bayonets*, Louisiana State University Press, 1965.

Murphy, Terrence V., *10th Virginia Infantry*, H. E. Howard, Inc., 1989.

National Archives, Military Service and Pensions Records, Washington, D.C.

Nevins, Allan, editor, *A Diary of Battle: The Personal Journals of Colonel Charles S. Wainwright, 1861–1865*, Da Capo Press, 1962.

Nye, Wibur S., *Here Come the Rebels!*, reprint by Morningside Bookshop, 1988.

Pfanz, Donald C., *Richard S. Ewell: A Soldier's Life*, University of North Carolina Press, 1998.

Pfanz, Harry W., *Gettysburg: Culp's Hill and Cemetery Hill*, University of North Carolina Press, 1993.

———. *"Old Jack" Is Not Here, The Gettysburg Nobody Knows*, editor Boritt, Gabor S., Oxford University Press, 1997.

———. *Gettysburg—The First Day*, University of North Carolina Press, 2001.

Raus, Edmund J. Jr., *A Generation on the March: The Union Army at Gettysburg*, Thomas Publications, 1996.

Sauers, Richard A., editor, *Fighting Them Over: How the Veterans Remembered Gettysburg in the Pages of the National Tribune*, Butternut and Blue, 1998.

———. *A Caspian Sea of Ink: The Meade-Sickles Controversy*, Butternut and Blue, 1989.

Sears, Stephen W., *Chancellorsville*, Houghton Mifflin Company, 1996.

Shevchuk, Paul M., *The Fight for Brinkerhoff's Ridge, July 2, 1863*, Gettysburg Magazine, January 1990.

*The Wounding of Albert Jenkins, July 2, 1863*, Gettysburg Magazine, July 1990.

Southern Historical Society Papers, ed. J. William Jones et al., 52 vols., 1877–1959, reprint with 3 volume index, Wilmington, N.C., 1990–1992.

Storrs, John W., *The Twentieth Connecticut, A Regimental History*, Ansonia, CT, 1886.

Taylor, Walter H., *Four Years with General Lee*, Indiana University Press, 1996.

Tevis, C. V., and Marquis, D. R., *The History of the Fighting Fourteenth: Red-Legged Devils*, 1911, reprinted by Butternut and Blue, 1994.

Tucker, Glenn, *High Tide at Gettysburg*, Stan Clark Military Books, 1958, reprinted 1995.

U.S. Army Military History Institute, Carlisle Barracks, Carlisle, Pennsylvania.

United States War Department, *The War of the Rebellion: A Compilation of the Official Records of the Union and Confederate Armies*, 128 volumes. Washington, DC: U.S. Government

Printing Office, 1880–1901, Reprinted by Morningside Bookshop, 1993.

Warner, Ezra J., *Generals in Blue: Lives of Union Commanders,* Baton Rouge, Louisiana State University Press, 1964.

————. *Generals in Gray: Lives of Confederate Commanders,* Baton Rouge, Louisiana State University Press, 1959.

Williams, Alpheus S., *From the Cannon's Mouth,* edited by Gallagher, Gary W., Bison Books, 1995.

Williams, T. Harry, *Selected Writings and Speeches of Abraham Lincoln,* Hendricks House, Inc., 1980.

Wise, Jennings Cropper, *The Long Arm of Lee,* 2 volumes, Bison Books, University of Nebraska Press, 1991.

# INDEX

177

# Index